Landmarks of world literature

THE BIBLE

Landmarks of world literature

General Editor: J. P. Stern

The Bible

STEPHEN PRICKETT
*Regius Professor of English
University of Glasgow*

and

ROBERT BARNES
*Lecturer in Religious Studies
Australian National University, Canberra*

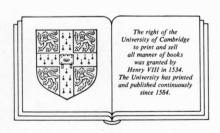

The right of the
University of Cambridge
to print and sell
all manner of books
was granted by
Henry VIII in 1534.
The University has printed
and published continuously
since 1584.

CAMBRIDGE UNIVERSITY PRESS
*Cambridge
New York   Port Chester
Melbourne   Sydney*

Published by the Press Syndicate of the University of Cambridge
The Pitt Building, Trumpington Street, Cambridge CB2 1RP
40 West 20th Street, New York, NY 10011-4211, USA
10 Stamford Road, Oakleigh, Melbourne 3166, Australia

© Cambridge University Press 1991

First published 1991

Printed in Great Britain at the University Press, Cambridge

British Library cataloguing in publication data
Prickett, Stephen
The Bible. − (Landmarks of world literature).
1. Bible. Literary aspects
I. Title   II. Barnes, Robert   III. Series
809.93522

Library of Congress cataloguing in publication data
Prickett, Stephen.
The Bible / Stephen Prickett and Robert Barnes.
  p.   cm. − (Landmarks of world literature)
Includes bibliographical references.
ISBN 0 521 36569 4. − ISBN 0 521 36759 X (paperback)
1. Bible − Introductions. I. Barnes, Robert. II. Title.
III. Series.
BS475.2.P75   1991
220.6′.1 − dc20   90–26059   CIP

ISBN 0 521 36569 4 hardback
ISBN 0 521 36759 X paperback

This book is dedicated to Maria, Mary, Tanya and Harab al-Shams

Contents

Preface

The original plan for the Landmarks of World Literature series envisaged separate volumes for the Hebrew Bible and the New Testament. The present authors have persuaded the series editor to accept instead a single volume on the whole Bible. In doing this they are not trying to make any case for the Christian Bible of Old and New Testaments as against the Jewish or Hebrew Bible. They do, however, believe that it is the 'whole' Bible which has become the 'landmark of world literature'; and that the New Testament is in essential literary continuity with the Hebrew Bible, without being its inevitable completion, or sole interpretative key.

This book is not intended as a critical introduction to the Bible, covering all the questions which such a title would imply; and for that reason, while it does suggest some general directions of modern biblical scholarship, it does not usually document them (several such introductions, with extensive documentation, are listed in the 'Guide to further reading'). It *does* try to place the Bible briefly in its original literary setting; it indicates its general contents and literary forms, and some of its themes; and it gives a very selective history of its interpretation and of its place in later literature.

Quotations from the Bible, except where otherwise indicated, are based on the Revised Standard Version, with regular change of 'the Lord' in the Hebrew Bible to 'Yahweh', and of 'thou' to 'you'. The former change is of course debatable, and contrary to the normal Jewish and Christian traditions of translation, but we believe that it should be made clear when the original text is using the particular name of the God of Israel.

We would particularly like to thank Ward Allen, for communicating some of his unrivalled knowledge of the history of the Authorized Version; parts of chapter 5 are heavily indebted to him; and to thank David Lawton, for giving us access to the manuscript of his important new book *Faith, Text and History: The Bible in English*; chapters 4 and 5 have benefited as a result. The section on literal and allegorical interpretations in chapter 4, section 4 is heavily indebted to Marjorie Reeves' 'The Bible and Literary Authorship in the Middle Ages' (*Reading the Text: Biblical Criticism and Literary Theory*, ed. Stephen Prickett, Oxford, Blackwell, 1991). Parts of chapters 1, 4, and 5 have appeared in a somewhat different form in *Literature and Criticism: a New Century Guide*, ed. M. Coyle, P. Garside, M. Kelsall, and J. Peck, London, Routledge, 1990. We are grateful to the publishers for their permission to use the material involved.

A time chart

BC

1200   Emergence of Israel
        Period of 'Judges'

1100

1000   Founding of Israelite monarchy by Saul
        David as King, Jerusalem taken as capital
        Solomon as King, Temple built in Jerusalem
        Divided monarchy of 'Judah' and 'Israel'

900

        Period of Elijah

800

        Period of Amos and Hosea
        722   Fall of Samaria, capital of Israel, to Assyrians

700   Period of Isaiah
        621   Under King Josiah, 'discovery' of
                Deuteronomy

600   Writing of 'Deuteronomistic History', period of
        Jeremiah
        586   Fall of Jerusalem, capital of Judah, to
                Babylonians
        Exile of Israelites in Babylonia, period of Ezekiel
        539   Conquest of Babylonia by Cyrus, Israelites'
                return

500   Period of Persian rule in Palestine, rebuilding
        of Temple
        Period of Ezra and Nehemiah

400   Editing of Pentateuch
        Alexander the Great conquers East

300   Palestine part of Greek Kingdom of Egypt

200   Palestine part of Greek Kingdom of Syria
       Maccabean uprising against Greek Kings of Syria
       Writing of Daniel

100

       63   Romans conquer Palestine
       37–4   Herod the Great as King of the Jews

AD

       c. 30   Death of Jesus
       50–60   Epistles of Paul
       60–90   Writing of Gospels

100

       Last books of New Testament written

200

Chapter 1

Introduction

The book

The world's largest theological libraries, such as the Andover-Harvard Theological Library and the Union Theological Seminary Library in New York, contain hundreds of thousands of works devoted in one way or another to the Bible and its contents. One can only guess, from publishers' catalogues and circulars, at the rate at which these collections must be growing in size every year. Publication mega-statistics are, of course, no final guide to a book's importance – during the Cultural Revolution in China *The Thoughts of Chairman Mao*, we are told, was distributed in such quantities as to make it the world's number one bestseller – but they do serve to highlight the scale of the present book in relation to its subject. The Bible is, simply in cultural terms, the most important single book in the history of Western civilization, if not of the world.

Our word 'Bible' is derived, via the French *bible*, from the late Latin *biblia*, a feminine singular noun meaning simply 'the (single) book'. In earlier Latin, however, *biblia* was not taken to be the feminine singular, but the neuter plural form, which, following the Greek, *ta biblia*, meant 'the (individual) books'. It was originally in fact no more than a physical description of the form in which the biblical texts were commonly held, before the invention of the codex: a collection of separate scrolls which would be stored in a wooden chest or cupboard. But that literal designation has had incalculable consequences. Right from the start, however accidentally, our sense of what the Bible is has contained a tension between singularity and pluralism, between unity and diversity. The Bible was 'the Book of Books': an ambiguous phrase implying that it was a collection of works somehow contributing to a mysterious unity greater than the sum of its parts, and, at the same time, *the* pre-eminent and superlative book – as it were the class-definer, the book by which all other books were to be known *as books*. The importance of this for the development of European literature and thought cannot be over–estimated. The Bible is, in short, a 'landmark' of world literature in a quite different sense from any other book.

Largely because of our biblical heritage, right from the late Roman Empire we have been accustomed culturally to thinking of books – all books – in certain ways. To begin with, we have learned to expect to discover in a story narrative rather than chronicle; there is a meaning to the whole cycle of human existence, both individual and collective; and each individual event, however seemingly trivial, has a figurative, typological, or, as we would now say, symbolic relation to the whole. This expectation runs very deep in Western society, affecting not merely fiction, but biography, history, and, of course, science – that distinctive product of a belief in a rational stable universe in which every part has its meaning in relation to the 'story' of the whole.

Secondly, and directly following from this, our idea of what constitutes a book includes within itself that notion of unity with diversity. We accept as normal many related parts: sub-plot and main-plot, stories within stories, parallel, complementary, even contradictory, stories that may connect thematically rather than by direct interaction.

Thirdly, we are accustomed to the idea that a book is in its very essence interpretative. In this, the Christian Bible, with its Old and New Testaments, differs in degree, but not essentially in kind, from the Jewish. At its very inception Christianity was faced with the task of reinterpreting the Israelite past. This act of appropriating and reinterpreting the Hebrew Bible (with some re-arrangement) as the 'Old Testament' presented a special problem. In its literal sense, much of the Old Testament bore little or no relation to the superstructure that was now being constructed upon it. In many cases, indeed, its narratives and even ethical teachings actually seemed to contradict those of the New Testament. Some method had to be found to harmonize the existing written tradition — which was, of course, held to be divinely inspired — with what was now believed to be its fulfilment. The early Church did this not by inventing an entirely new technique, but by developing an exegetical tradition already at work in the Hebrew Bible. The interpretation of texts was thus not an incidental activity of the new religion, but an essential part of its foundation and subsequent development. In this sense at least, critical theory was what Christianity was concerned with.

Yet just because Christianity began with a special sense that it differed from the world that preceded it, and that its own heritage had to be thought of differently from the way in which it had hitherto been understood, the interpretative function of narrative was uniquely central right from the start. When the Greek historian Herodotus visited Thebes in Egypt, he gazed with awe at 300 generations of high priests of the Theban temple listed in its inscriptions, as he realized that they went back for thousands of years before the dawn of Greek history. J. H. Plumb has contrasted this disturbing experience, that began to give meaning and shape to the idea of history for the Greeks, with the untroubled serenity of the Chinese chroniclers, for whom the succession of one emperor after another for upwards of 5000 years was simply a sequence of time (*The Death of the Past*, London, 1969, p. 111). In contrast with the Chinese, the compilers of the New Testament, like Herodotus, saw in the past not a sequence of events, but a problem with a meaning that had to be explained.

This sense of the past as a problem was compounded by the events of the first few centuries of the Christian era. One reason, perhaps, why Christianity, rather than its many rivals, was able to ride out the destruction of the Roman Empire was that it already contained within its own literature models not merely for the destruction of empires, but for a *meaningful* pattern to their rise and fall. The biblical world was never a monoculture existing in isolation from surrounding societies. On the contrary, it clung to a marginal existence at the intersection of great powers, and Jewish political and cultural life flowered only in the brief intervals between the waning and waxing of the imperial ambitions of others — Egyptians, Assyrians, Babylonians, Persians, Greeks, and Romans.

This leads us to our fourth point about the expectations of a book inherent in our biblically based culture. It is one best expressed in the technical jargon of literary theory: intertextuality. Europe's past is rooted in a translated book — not merely a translation for modern Europeans, but essentially and in its very origins. Though it is presented as arising from the very peculiar experience of one particular people, the Bible is in fact a palimpsest of languages and contexts. Thus, though the Old Testament is written almost entirely in Hebrew, substantial parts of it incorporate translation or paraphrase of other Near Eastern texts — Mesopotamian, Egyptian, Canaanite, and others. By New Testament times, however, Hebrew had fallen out of use as a vernacular language, and in synagogues the Hebrew Bible had to be explained even to Jewish congregations by Aramaic paraphrases, called Targums, or, in Greek-speaking areas, by the Septuagint. Though Jesus presumably spoke in the Palestinian Jewish vernacular of his time, Aramaic, the Gospel tradition survives only as a Greek translation — in the popular form of the language of a classical and centralizing high culture. Some scholars have even argued that Jesus himself was Greek-speaking. Certainly most of the early Christians, after perhaps only the first generation, lost almost all contact with the Semitic biblical languages, Hebrew and Aramaic, and for them the Old Testament was henceforth either the Septuagint, or, later, the Old Latin, and finally the Vulgate versions. If we were prepared to accept the controversial argument of G. B. Caird that Hebrew was in fact the traditional language not of the Jews, but of the Canaanites, and, yet more controversially, that Aramaic was none other than the original Israelite vernacular (*The Language and Imagery of the Bible*, London, 1980, p. 35), we would have yet another illustration of the essentially intertextual nature of the Bible's construction. Because it has taken its very existence from the intersection of other languages and cultures, the Bible has always been at once marginal and assimilative: culturally meek but fully prepared to inherit the earth.

It follows from this, of course, that questions of translation have always been inseparable from questions of interpretation. As we shall see in the specific case of the history of the English Bible in chapter 5, for Renaissance scholars the actual words of the Greek and Hebrew were vitally important; modern translators, on the other hand, have tended to think in terms of the concepts and experiences that seem to them to be described in the Bible, rather than the precise words in which they are conveyed. Both attitudes conceal interpretative assumptions: for the Renaissance it was obvious that, if the words of scripture were dictated by the Holy Spirit (whatever subsequent transmission problems may have arisen through translation or copying), the major problem lay in discovering the exact meanings of those words; for modern translators it seems to be equally obvious that the biggest problems concern not the language itself so much as our cultural distance from the mental worlds and social settings of the original writers.

Given this heritage, it is hardly surprising that literary criticism itself, as we now know it, had its origins in the study of the Bible. That is to say, European literary criticism, like its sense of history, was born of a problem that did not affect the other great classical literary cultures of India and China. That problem centred on the relationship between the biblical writings and the classical literature of Greece and Rome. It was a problem that, for instance, had worried both Augustine and Jerome. To quote Plumb again: 'History began because scholars perceived a problem which faced no other civilization – the problem of the duality of Europe's past, its conflicting ideologies and of their different interpretations of human destiny' (*Death of the Past*, p. 136).

From the exploration of that problem was to stem, not merely our peculiar sense of history, but many of the great questions of Western philosophy as well. Thus our sense of a book is shaped by the existence of the Bible in very particular and highly complex ways. So central are these to our own culture, that it is only by a very self-conscious effort that we can focus on them at all. We shall be looking, for instance, in chapter 4, at causes and implications of the contemporary crisis over the historicity of biblical narrative − a crisis that is reflected not least by the tacit assumption of Cambridge University Press, in the 1990s, that the Bible is a work of literature worthy of inclusion in a series of books on the great 'landmarks' of world literature. This, in itself, indicates something of the radical change in status undergone by the Bible in relatively recent times. Nor is it the first such change.

The Jewish and Christian Bibles

It should be clear from what has already been said that questions of its interpretation cannot be separated from the most apparently neutral descriptions of the Bible. This is true even of such a simple question as 'what is the Bible?' The format and arrangement of the book as it sits in front of us is itself a matter of hermeneutics ('hermeneutics' being the science of interpretation of literary texts). The Christian appropriation of the Hebrew Bible as the Old Testament, for instance, in spite of comparatively few changes in the actual writings involved, nevertheless totally transformed their status. Though Christians eventually settled on a somewhat expanded canon (or list of books accepted as comprising the Bible), it was in the ordering and relative importance given to the various sections of the canon that the real change was felt.

The Hebrew Bible is traditionally divided into three sections: the *Torah* (the five books of Moses, corresponding to what Christians call the Pentateuch); the *Prophets* (divided into the 'Former Prophets', i.e. the 'histories' from Joshua to Kings, but not including Ruth, Esther, Chronicles, or Ezra-Nehemiah; and the 'Latter Prophets', or what Christians call the 'Prophets' simply); and a final section known as *Writings*, which includes the Psalms, Proverbs, Job, the five Megilloth or 'Scrolls' (Song of Songs, Ruth, Lamentations, Ecclesiastes, Esther), and Daniel, and ends with Ezra-Nehemiah and Chronicles. The Old Testament of the Christian Bible, however, is commonly divided into four sections: the *Pentateuch*; the

Histories (including Joshua to Kings, with Ruth following Judges, Chronicles, Ezra, Nehemiah, and Esther); the *Poetical Books* (Job, Psalms, Proverbs, Ecclesiastes, and the Song of Songs); and the *Prophets* (including Daniel). The difference of interpretation implied by these arrangements is striking. For Jews, the Torah is the foundational document both of the Bible and of their own people; the histories from Joshua to the fall of the monarchy are combined with the prophetic texts as a historical illustration of what the prophets promised and threatened; and the Writings are a somewhat open-ended group of texts, related in various ways to the practice of the Jewish religion after the Babylonian exile. For Christians, all the historical texts of the Old Testament go together, as it were placing the history of Israel firmly in the past; the poetical books tend to be seen timelessly, and are frequently drawn on for prayer and meditation; and the prophets come last, pointing to the future and the fulfilment of the Old Testament in the New.

The arrangement of the Hebrew Bible appears to be significant in more detailed ways as well. The ending of the Torah, for instance, with the death of Moses outside the Promised Land, rather than including the Book of Joshua and the triumphant conquest of Canaan, is a clear hermeneutic signal of a kind. It has been seen as part of the pattern of perpetual exile and questing that has characterized the Jewish people for thousands of years – contrasting sharply with the more clearly organized pattern of a closed history of the old Israel, and prophecy of a new one, in the Christian understanding of the Old Testament. Even before we come to the New Testament, the Christian arrangement of the Old is not accidental, but a polemical and even a doctrinal pointer to what lies ahead of it.

The basic arrangement of the New Testament, when its contents were finally settled, also illustrates the essentially literary and self-referential nature of the Bible's construction. Thus the four Gospels – Matthew, Mark, Luke, and John – are placed together, and identified (at least from the time of Irenaeus of Lyon in the late second century AD) with the 'four living creatures' of Revelation 4:6ff., which were themselves based on the 'four living creatures' of Ezekiel 1. The Acts of the Apostles, also supposedly written by Luke, is a continuation of his Gospel. The 'fourteen' Epistles traditionally attributed to Paul are grouped with the 'Catholic' Epistles of James, Peter, John, and Jude. Last comes the Apocalypse, or Book of Revelation, also supposedly written by the same John. The hermeneutic signal of this arrangement is clear: in the Gospels we are to see the coming of the prophesied Messiah of Israel, and his founding of the new Israel, the church. In Acts we are to see the spread of this new Israel from the centre of the old, in Jerusalem, to the centre of the new world, in Rome. In the Epistles we are instructed on how the church is to conduct itself in the world, pending the return of the Messiah. In Revelation we have visions of the church's trials and temptations in the world, brought to a glorious end with the fall of Babylon (= Rome), the final defeat of Satan, the descent of the new Jerusalem from heaven, and its marriage to the Lamb. Thus, though the New Testament completes the Old, it may be more correct to say that, in many ways, it is a continuation of it: its concepts and imagery are essentially those of the Hebrew Bible, which it at all times presupposes and makes no claims to supersede; and its visions of the end, like those of the Hebrew Bible, are really just that: visions, not predictions. It is that continuity that is the central theme of this book.

The Bible: the circumstances of its writing

The Hebrew Bible is the main surviving literature of the people of ancient Israel. The origins of this people are much debated: the Bible's own accounts in Genesis of God's choice of Abraham, and of his promises to Abraham of land and descendants, are legendary, and irrelevant to the kind of reconstruction which modern historians find satisfactory. The same can be said of the accounts in Exodus of God's revelation of his name 'Yahweh' to Moses, of Moses' leading of the Israelites out of Egypt, and of the covenant made by God, through Moses, with the Israelites at Mount Sinai. Even the accounts in the Book of Joshua of a systematic conquest of the land of Palestine by the Israelites under Joshua seem to be largely legendary (partly because the details of the accounts are often hard to reconcile with archaeological discoveries at the cities mentioned as being conquered). Many scholars therefore rely on non-biblical data for reconstructing the early history of Israel, particularly archaeological data from Palestine, but also any relevant (or apparently relevant) references in Egyptian and other ancient written sources. Such data suggest that 'Israel' emerged as a separate people by about 1200 BC, perhaps largely made up of refugee peasants and workers fleeing into highland areas of Palestine from oppressive conditions in the Canaanite city-states of the region, but perhaps also gradually joined by nomadic or semi-nomadic groups, whose traditions, including traditions of an escape from bondage in Egypt, eventually contributed to the later Israelite belief that the people as a whole were immigrants.

This people slowly occupied or conquered much of the territory of their former oppressors, and at some stage their different groups emerged as tribes (normally thought to be twelve in number, though the details of the names vary in different lists), each occupying specific areas. Certain events of this tribal period seem to be reflected in the Book of Judges, though the extent to which the tribal leaders who are the heroes of that book were ever accepted as 'judges' of all of Israel is uncertain. About 1000 BC the tribes were forced, by pressures from other surrounding peoples such as the Philistines, to unite in a monarchy. After Saul's shaky start, King David, and his son King Solomon, established a more or less unified state, with its capital at Jerusalem. The rise of the monarchy is narrated in the Books of Samuel, though with many legendary elements; and archaeological evidence does not suggest that the state of Israel at this time was as prosperous or as geographically extended as the Books of Samuel and Kings picture it.

After Solomon's death, the ten northern tribes broke away under Jeroboam I to form the 'Kingdom of Israel', with its capital eventually at Samaria, while the remaining two southern tribes of Judah and Benjamin formed the 'Kingdom of Judah'. The northern Kingdom survived, through several dynasties, until Samaria was conquered by the Assyrians, in 722/1 BC, and its people partly dispersed; the southern Kingdom survived, under the 'House of David', until Jerusalem was conquered finally by the Babylonians in 587/6, and its leaders were taken into captivity in Mesopotamia. These events, from the accession of Solomon, are narrated in the Books of Kings. Despite many uncertain details in these books, and despite apparently legendary elements, especially in the account of Solomon (e.g. the story of his judgement between two prostitutes in I Kings 3, and the accounts of his riches and wisdom in I Kings 10), the narrative framework of the books seems essentially reliable, and parts of it are confirmed by other sources from the ancient Near East.

Any account of the rise of the Israelite people must, of course, also try to account for the rise of Israelite religion. The Bible's own evidence on this is complex, and partly contradictory. According to Genesis 2:26, 'men began to call on the name of Yahweh' in the earliest generations. However, in Exodus 3 God only reveals his name to Moses at Sinai, shortly before Moses leads the Israelites out of Egypt, and he 'explains' his name, by way of a sort of folk etymology, as meaning 'I am who I am'. This passage, like the Pentateuch as a whole, reflects a later Israelite belief that their religion in all its detail was revealed to Moses, whereas many modern scholars assume a more gradual development of the religion, closely related to the general development of Israelite society. The ultimate origin of the name 'Yahweh' is still unclear, though it may be related to a similar name for a place in the Negev or Sinai area mentioned in Egyptian sources of the fourteenth and thirteenth centuries BC, and the cult of Yahweh bears some similarity to other cults known from the same area. Presumably the more or less exclusive religion of Yahweh provided the ideological motivation for the emergence of Israel as a people, and for such unity as the Israelite tribes achieved (partly by way of central Yahwistic shrines at Shechem, Shiloh, and elsewhere), as well as for the final establishment of a monarchy.

However, the Bible itself suggests that the Israelites were always torn between exclusive devotion to Yahweh and com-

promise with the Canaanite religion of their neighbours – a
dilemma made all the more acute by the fact that Yahwistic
religion itself had from the start, and inevitably in the circumstances, accepted many features of Canaanite religion
without question. During the monarchy the 'prophets of
Yahweh' are presented as the great champions of exclusive
Yahwism, but they are regularly shown as being in conflict with
'prophets of Baal' or 'false prophets' from among their own
people. We now know, from other ancient Near Eastern
sources, that various forms of prophecy existed in the area long
before the time of Israel – i.e. direct communications of gods
to humans, relayed by an intermediary 'prophet'. (The examples that seem closest to Israelite prophecy are those mentioned in the 'Mari Letters' to King Zimri-Lim, which were
buried in his palace at Mari on the Euphrates when it was
destroyed by Hammurabi of Babylon in the eighteenth century BC.) We also know that many details of the royal
patronage of the Yahweh cult, including the form of the
Jerusalem temple, and much to do with its sacrifices and other
ritual, were normal for the period. Even Yahweh's promises
to David, the essence of the ideology of Zion and of Israelite
Messianism, bear close resemblances to other religio-political
rhetoric of the day.

There is no surviving evidence that the earliest Israelites were
literate, and it is commonly assumed that the first Israelite
literature dates from the monarchy (though of course this
literature was partly based on older oral traditions). Until
recently, most followers of 'biblical criticism' claimed to discern
continuous strands in the Pentateuch of the Bible. These were
called J, E, D, and P, with the J, or 'Yahwistic', strand dating
from the early monarchy and becoming the standard history
of early Israel for the southern kingdom of Judah; the E, or
'Elohistic', strand being the corresponding standard history for
the northern kingdom of Israel; the D material (essentially the
Book of Deuteronomy) coming from the late southern
kingdom; and the P strand reflecting a 'Priestly' editing and
expansion of the older strands during and after the Babylonian exile. At present this claim is being hotly debated (it will

be discussed below, see pp. 98–101). It seems to some contemporary scholars that the 'sources' of the Pentateuch were actually much more complex and piecemeal than this documentary theory claims, and possibly also that few of them were written at all until towards the end of the monarchy, or even later. It has been suggested, for example, that the stories about Abraham in Genesis, far from being first written down in the early monarchy but reflecting the social and political conditions of 1000 years earlier, in fact reflect the conditions of the sixth century BC, with the promises of land to Abraham being an ideological claim to the land of Palestine at a time when the Israelites had been largely exiled from it (John Van Seters, *Abraham in History and Tradition*, New Haven, Connecticut, 1975).

However, it is certain, at least, that the earliest stages of the Israelite literary tradition date from the time of the monarchy, that is, from some time between 1000 and 586 BC. Like so many other aspects of Israelite culture in this period, its literature bears many resemblances (as well as some striking differences) to other literatures of the ancient Near East. The biblical legal codes, such as the 'Book of the Covenant' in Exodus 21–3, the 'Holiness Code' in Leviticus 17–28, and Deuteronomy 12–26, are similar in many respects to various Sumerian, Babylonian, and other codes. Yet even here there are significant inversions of emphasis. Whereas these other codes were usually promulgated by particular kings, such as Hammurabi in Babylon, the biblical codes, on the contrary, are presented as God's requirements from the Israelites as part of his covenant with them. The hymns and prayers of the Bible can be seen as parallel in form, structure, and imagery with Mesopotamian, Canaanite, and Egyptian prayers, but the exclusive monotheism of Yahwistic religion in Israel is also very clear in such texts. The primeval history of Genesis 1–11 includes many more or less mythological features which have a long history in the religions of the Near East (and there is even a sort of parallel to the primeval history as a whole in the Akkadian Atrahasis Epic), but again the Yahwistic view of God considerably modifies such features.

There are scattered parallels to the stories of Abraham, Isaac, Jacob, Joseph, and Moses in Genesis and Exodus, and to a number of the stories in Samuel and Kings; and there is a sort of parallel to the dual history of the kings of Israel and Judah in Kings in the 'Assyrian Synchronistic History'. However, there are no real parallels in the ancient Near East to the consolidated large-scale history writing of the Israelites: it has been suggested recently that the ancient Greek historical tradition, effectively beginning with Herodotus, is a much closer parallel, and that both the Israelite and the Greek historical traditions are reflections of fundamentally democratic societies (John Van Setters, *In Search of History: Historiography in the Ancient World and the Origins of Biblical History*, New Haven, Connecticut, 1983). Various forms of prophecy were fairly widespread in the ancient Near East, but there are only very partial parallels to the collected books of the prophets in the Bible. Finally, the Israelite 'wisdom literature', in such books as Proverbs, Job and Ecclesiastes, has many parallels (sometimes very close parallels) in other Near Eastern literatures; but again the exclusive nature of Yahwistic religion gives the Israelite examples of such literature a distinct stamp. In the Books of Job and Ecclesiastes, for instance, the tension between the 'wise' and the Yahwistic outlooks has created poetic compositions which for many readers today are among the most timeless and moving parts of the Bible.

It is probably safe to assume that, when the political and religious leaders of Judah were exiled to Babylonia in 586, they could take with them the following parts of the Bible: some sort of historical framework for the Pentateuch, and perhaps whole sections, such as the Book of Deuteronomy, more or less in their present form; the major part of what modern scholars call the 'Deuteronomistic history', from Joshua to Kings; several collections of prophetic texts which had originally been assembled by disciples of the earlier prophets; and an uncertain number of Psalms, wisdom texts, and other writings. During the exile, until Cyrus, the King of Persia, conquered Babylon in 539 and allowed the Israelites and other deported peoples to return to their homelands, these texts seem to have been edited and expanded. They also gained a new significance as the main link between the scattered Israelites and their cultural past; perhaps, too, the notion that the sayings collected in the prophetic books were 'words of Yahweh' was gradually extended to the texts as a whole, so that eventually the whole literature was thought to be inspired. Several completely new works were added to Israelite literature during the exile, including Ezekiel and 'Second Isaiah', i.e. Isaiah 40–55 (with the final chapters of Isaiah, 56–66, being added after the exile).

In 538 BC a first group of Israelite exiles returned to Palestine. Between 520 and 515 the Temple was rebuilt in Jerusalem, and in these years the prophecies of Haggai and Zechariah were delivered. At a much later stage, probably 444 BC, Nehemiah, a Babylonian Jew and butler to the King of Persia, 'returned' to rebuild the walls of Jerusalem and enforce various religious practices there; and possibly at a later stage again, about 400 BC, Ezra, a Jewish priest and scribe, came from Babylon to read the 'Book of the Law of Moses' to the people in Jerusalem, and enforce Jewish religious practices even more strictly. (The dates of the missions of Ezra and Nehemiah are uncertain, because of what seem to be confusions in the Books of Ezra and Nehemiah.) At all events, the Book of the Law of Moses read by Ezra was probably some substantial part of the legal sections of the Pentateuch. There were further additions to Israelite literature after Ezra; and the Book of Daniel was apparently only written in its present form in the 160s BC; it was probably the last-written work to be included in the Hebrew canon of the Bible.

By the time the last works of the Hebrew Bible were written, Alexander the Great, King of Macedon, had conquered the whole of the Near East, and from then on Palestine was part of the Greek (and later the Roman) world. It seems that Hebrew had fallen out of use as the everyday language of the Israelites during the exile. Aramaic became the normal language of Palestine during the Persian period and continued as such in the more Jewish areas of the country even in the following Greek period, but Greek was the language of administration, and to some extent of the non-Jewish cities. This situation explains why the Old Testament is written in Hebrew (with a few passages in Aramaic), and why, although Jesus probably spoke Aramaic, his sayings have been preserved only in the Greek of the New Testament.

The dates of Jesus' life are perhaps from 4 BC to 30 AD. The New Testament was written between about 50 and 150 AD: the certainly genuine Epistles of Paul in the 50s, and the other 'Pauline' Epistles later; the Gospels and Acts between the 60s and 90s; Revelation perhaps in the 90s; and the other Epistles perhaps mainly from the 90s on. (There is, however, some case for placing Luke and Acts in this latest period also.) As with the Old Testament (see further below), the canonization of this literature was rather gradual. For Jesus and his immediate followers, the Bible was the Hebrew Bible. Only during the second century AD did the early Christian writings come to be thought of as scripture in the same sense as the Old Testament; and only considerably later was there more or less final agreement on exactly which Christian writings should be included as the New Testament. It should be noted here that the authors' names traditionally attached to the New Testament books are in most cases questionable: we can be fairly sure that Paul wrote at least some of the Epistles that bear his name (see further discussion of this below, pp. 33–42), and that one 'John' wrote Revelation, but otherwise these names seem to go back to second century AD traditions of uncertain value.

During the early Christian period there was also considerable debate about the canon of the Old Testament. The first certain evidence of a fixed canon of the Hebrew Bible appears in the writings of Josephus, the Jewish historian, late in the first century AD. However, there was almost certainly general agreement among most Jews from at least the second century BC that the scriptures included the Pentateuch, the so-called 'Former Prophets' (that is, the historical books from Joshua to Kings), the 'Latter Prophets' (what are normally called the Prophets in Christian Bibles), and at least some of the other 'Writings', such as the Psalms, Proverbs and Job. Just when and how Chronicles, Ezra, Nehemiah and Daniel came to be included is less certain. The five short Megilloth ('Scrolls') of the Song of Songs, Ruth, Lamentations, Ecclesiastes, and Esther were probably included because they were read on particular Jewish festivals.

This canon in effect excluded a large number of other Jewish works of the Greek period, variously written in Hebrew, Aramaic or Greek. Some of these, such as the Book of Wisdom, Ecclesiasticus (or the 'Wisdom of Ben Sirach'), Judith, and several Books of Maccabees, were eventually grouped as the Apocrypha of the Christian Bible. These have varying canonical status in different Christian churches; the Christian biblical scholar Jerome, who revised the Latin translations of the Bible in the fourth century AD to form the Vulgate, wished to follow the Hebrew canon and exclude them from the Bible; in this, however, he was not followed by the rest of the Christian tradition until the Reformation. A much larger body of such writings, often today called the Pseudepigrapha, was eventually excluded from all the canons of the Bible. It is a body continually being added to from such discoveries as the Dead Sea Scrolls, recovered in the years following 1947, which for modern scholars have greatly illuminated the background of the New Testament.

It was pointed out above that the Hebrew Bible can now be seen as closely related to other literatures of the ancient Near East. Similarly, the New Testament can be seen, not merely as intimately related to the Hebrew Bible and to other Jewish literature, but also against the background of Greek literature. At least in form, the Gospels appear to have much in common with the Greek biographical tradition. The Acts of the Apostles includes some of the trappings of Greek history writing of the Hellenistic period (though it also includes features of Greek novels or romances). The Epistles of the New Testament have much of the same structure as other letters of the Hellenistic world, both real, documentary letters, and literary letters; they also include certain well-known Greek rhetorical features of their period, and Paul's in particular seem to owe something to the 'diatribe', or popular Greek philosophical lecture.

The Bible, then, is a highly composite work, written over something like a 1000-year period, and reflecting much of the extremely complex political and cultural development of the Near East during that millennium. Its earliest parts are in a sort of dialogue with the earliest literate cultures of the world, those of Mesopotamia, the Levant and Egypt; its latest parts are equally in a dialogue with the Greco-Roman world. The Bible's extensive assimilation of those cultures, and partial rejection of them, were to be momentous factors in later Western cultural development.

Chapter 2

The contents of the Bible

This chapter summarizes the contents of the main books or sections of the Bible. For the Hebrew Bible the traditional Jewish order of books is followed, with some minor changes in the 'Writings'. For the New Testament the traditional order is followed, except that Mark, being commonly regarded as the earliest Gospel, is placed first. Discussions of sources and other critical matters are avoided, except where these are essential for understanding the present contents of the books. However, some general indication is given of ancient Near Eastern or Greek backgrounds, where these throw light on what sort of works the books are. Comments are also offered on books or sections which point backwards or forwards, in particularly important ways, to other parts of the Bible. The New Testament section begins with a short discussion of 'The Gospels and the historical Jesus'.

The Hebrew Bible

Genesis Genesis consists of two obviously different parts: the *Primeval History* in 1–11, and the *History of the Patriarchs* in 12–50. The *Primeval History* aims to give an account of the creation of the world and of human beings; of humans' frustrated desire to be like God; of the development of human culture from a hunting to an agricultural to a technological level; of the limitations on the span of life allowed to humans; of God's attempt to wipe out human beings by a flood while saving one man, Noah, and his family with the animals; of the racial groupings and diverse languages of mankind; and of the supposed generations of the first men down to the Hebrew patriarchs. This primeval history draws on many mythological elements from the ancient Israelites' cultural environment (at

18

the same time criticizing of them). It is a picture of primitive men which has contributed something to modern anthropological assumptions about human development; and of course it sets the scene for the history of the Israelites which is to follow. This begins with the *History of the Patriarchs* – Abraham, Isaac, Jacob (or 'Israel', taking the name of the whole later people), and Joseph. The materials in these stories are highly diverse, but they have been shown to correspond in many details to widespread legendary and folklore patterns. One recurring theme in the stories, which is no doubt intended to give a sort of direction to the whole history of Israel, is that of God's promises of land and descendants to the patriarchs. Another is the epiphanies, or manifestations, of God at various named places in Palestine, which serve to strengthen the claim of the God of the Israelites to the land. The story of Joseph, filling most of 37–50, is a rather more unified composition than the rest of the book. It has been called a romance, or novella, perhaps connected to the 'wisdom' strand in ancient Near Eastern literature, in that it shows the triumph of a wise young Israelite, Joseph, in the difficult conditions of a foreign country, Egypt. It also, of course, explains how the Israelites came to be in Egypt, where the following book takes up their story.

Exodus The hero of Exodus, Moses, is shown as being cast upon the waters as a child (being outcast, in some way, is a typical feature of hero stories in the ancient world), but then being found and brought up at the Egyptian court. He flees to Mount Sinai in the wilderness, where God reveals his name, Yahweh, to him, and announces his plan that Moses should lead the Israelites out of Egypt. After persuading Pharaoh to allow this, by means of the ten plagues, and after celebrating the first Passover with the Israelites, Moses leads them to the Sea of Reeds (this is a more accurate translation than 'Red Sea'), where the Egyptian army is drowned while trying to pursue them. He brings them to Sinai, where God makes a covenant with them, and in the rest of the book Moses receives from God much detail about the institutions of Israelite religion, in particular about how to construct and move a 'tent of meeting', which evidently foreshadows the later Temple in Jerusalem. This book is in many ways the central text of the Pentateuch, and the foundational text of the Bible: the story of the exodus from Egypt remains a key image throughout the Bible and a model for Israelite hopes, and the covenant at Sinai becomes the essential context for defining Israelite religion, as well as the model for the New 'Testament'. Moses is the lawgiver and mediator of the new religion to Israel, but also the first of the prophets; and all of these roles, as well as many details of Mosaic 'typology', will be attributed to Jesus. (Typology will be discussed below, see pp. 87–9.)

Leviticus, Numbers   Leviticus is devoted to the cultic and purity laws of the Israelite community. Here, as elsewhere in the Pentateuch, these laws are to be spoken by Moses to Israel. They are of considerable anthropological interest, and will be discussed further on pp. 62–5. Numbers narrates the end of the Israelites' sojourn at Sinai; their refusal to enter Palestine, as Caleb and Joshua urge them to do, because of their fear of the existing inhabitants; and their being condemned to wander in the wilderness of Paran for forty years, until this first faithless generation who had left Egypt has died out. There is also a series of events in Transjordan, including the prophet Balaam's refusal to curse the Israelites as they pass through Moab and the assignment of lands in Transjordan to two and a half of the Israelite tribes. The image of Israel wandering in the wilderness remains a powerful one throughout the Bible, both as a threat of what God might reduce his people to again, and as a condition of suffering from which he might lead them home.

Deuteronomy   The traditional title of this book, meaning 'second law', is taken from 17:18: 'And when he [the king whom the Israelites may choose to set over themselves] sits on the throne of his kingdom, he shall write for himself in a book a copy of this law . . .'. Whereas the other legal passages in the Pentateuch are 'to be spoken' by Moses to the people, Deuteronomy is presented as his actual speech, shortly before his death, to the new generation of Israelites who are about to cross into Palestine. This change of circumstances is no doubt a signal to the readers that this is to be more than a repetition of what they already know. Many modern scholars believe, as did some ancient ones, that Deuteronomy is in fact the 'book of the law' said, in II Kings 22:8, to have been found in the Temple of Jerusalem in the eighteenth year of King Josiah's reign (perhaps 621 BC), and used by Josiah as the basis for an exclusive Yahwistic religious reform in Israel. This would probably mean that it was in fact written towards the end of the monarchy, and it may well have been the first such comprehensive code to be written. The book contains two introductory speeches by Moses, in chapters 1–11, which rehearse God's deeds to the Israelites and exhort them to follow this God alone and his commandments. These are in a highly affective rhetorical style, which can still easily move modern readers; this style reappears in many parts of the actual code, in chapters 12–28. The book ends with several final exhortations and blessings from Moses, and an account of his death. The book is at once the conclusion and the summing up of the Pentateuch, the theological key to understanding the very mixed history of Israel which is to follow, and a continually new law for whenever Israel chooses to return to God. Not surprisingly, there will be many allusions to it in the New Testament.

Joshua, Judges These books begin the 'Former Prophets', in Jewish terminology, and the 'Deuteronomistic History' of modern scholars. The latter term indicates that the historical books, from Joshua to Kings, seem to have been written, or at least extensively edited, according to the exclusive Yahwistic outlook of Deuteronomy. If the latter is indeed a product of the later monarchy, then the Deuteronomistic History would come from near the end of the monarchy (with a further revision during the exile, to take into account the fall of Jerusalem to the Babylonians). We naturally tend to assume that it was written after the Pentateuch, which deals with 'earlier' events and is traditionally attributed to Moses, but quite possibly the Deuteronomistic History was in fact the earlier work to reach substantially its present form, and Genesis to Numbers were then rewritten, during or even after the exile, from varied existing materials, to be a sort of prologue to the work. If this *was* the case, then the attribution of the Pentateuch to Moses would represent a re-interpretation of this prologue as in fact the more central text. At all events, Joshua contains, first, an account of the conquest of Palestine by the Israelites under Joshua, then details of the division of the land among the tribes, and finally, in 23–4, a sort of renewal of God's covenant with Israel at Shechem (which in fact does not mention the earlier covenant at Sinai, one of many signs that the Bible's order of events in the history of early Israel may have been imposed on originally unrelated traditions). Judges, though it begins with a summary of the Israelite occupation of Palestine very different from the one given in Joshua, 'continues' this history. The stories it contains come from many different tribal traditions, but the 'Deuteronomistic' writer or editor of the book has imposed on them a common pattern: first there is a period of obedience to Yahweh, which brings prosperity; then the people's obedience slackens; their disobedience weakens the faith which alone can keep the community together; their enemies attack them; they repent, and a particular 'judge' is raised up by God to defend them. This pattern might be called the Deuteronomist's theology of history; with variations it recurs through Samuel and Kings as well. Judges includes, in 13–16, as its largest single element, the story of the hero Samson. Gabriel Josipovici, in his *The Book of God: a Response to the Bible* (New Haven, Connecticut, 1988), very appropriately titles his chapter on Judges 'The Rhythm Falters'.

Samuel Samuel and Kings are divided and named somewhat differently in different strands of the biblical tradition; the normal modern practice follows the Hebrew tradition. The two Books of Samuel cover the stories of Samuel (in some ways the last of the 'judges', but also presented as a prophet and priest); of his anointing of Saul as first King of Israel; of Saul's failure to defend Israel against the Philistines, and his death at their hands; of David's rise to power and eventual choice by the tribes as King of Israel; of his capture of Jerusalem from the Jebusites; and of his family and reign. One section of particular interest is I Samuel 8–12, where we are given both anti- and pro-monarchical accounts of the anointing of Saul. These may, as often suggested, reflect different sources; but more importantly they express very vividly the ambiguity over the monarchy which we find throughout these historical books. Another striking section is the story of the succession to David in II Samuel 9–20 and I Kings 1f., a unified composition in a distinctive and elegant narrative style. Despite its tales of rape and treachery among David's sons, it is remarkably free of Deuteronomistic moral comment (except perhaps for Nathan's rebuke of David in 12). It might therefore be a fairly late addition to the rest of the history, and if so makes an alternative, comparatively amoral and realistic comment on that history.

Kings The two Books of Kings continue the history of the Israelite monarchy from the reign of Solomon, through the split of the monarchy into the northern Kingdom of Israel and the southern Kingdom of Judah, to the fall of Israel to the Assyrians, and the fall of Judah to the Babylonians. The reign of Solomon is presented as a time of legendary wealth, and Solomon himself as possessed of legendary wisdom. However, the Deuteronomist adds, in I Kings 11, that Solomon's many 'foreign women' 'turned away his heart after other gods; and his heart was not wholly true to Yahweh his God, as was the heart of David his father'. This note recurs repeatedly in the remainder of Kings. Also recurring, and closely related to judgements on the Yahwistic orthodoxy of the kings, are stories about prophets: on the one side, the prophets of Yahweh – Elijah, Elisha, Micah and Isaiah – urge the kings to follow the commandments of Yahweh, and correctly predict the future; and on the other, 'false' and deluded prophets mislead kings and people with promises of success. The Deuteronomist gives a straightforward and lengthy judgement on the fall of the northern monarchy in II Kings 17: 'And this was so because the people of Israel had sinned against Yahweh their God . . . and walked in the customs of the nations whom Yahweh drove out before the people of Israel, and in the customs which the kings of Israel had introduced'. Quite possibly this judgement comes from a first edition of the Deuteronomistic history, written to warn the southern kingdom while it still remained of what might happen to it too unless it mended its ways. During the exile there would then have appeared a second edition which narrated, in II Kings 24–5, the fall of the southern monarchy to the Babylonians. Interestingly, II Kings 24:3ff. blames this fall on Yahweh's continuing resentment against the sins of Manasseh, a king actually earlier than Josiah, under whom the first edition is most likely to have been written. The second edition is thus saying 'it was in fact already too late for Josiah to avert Yahweh's anger'. The actual fall, and the exile, are narrated without further comment, which was presumably now superfluous. However, the book ends, intriguingly, with a mention that the king of Babylon 'graciously freed Jehoiachin king of Judah from prison'; the writer's hope was not quite dead even now.

Isaiah   Isaiah is the first of the 'Latter Prophets' in the Jewish tradition, or simply the 'Prophets' in the Christian tradition. Isaiah was part of an older succession of Yahwistic prophets, but he is the first of the prophets named there whose prophecies survive as an independent collection in the Bible, and, roughly, a contemporary of Amos, Hosea and Micah, whose prophecies also survive. The Book of Isaiah, however, is a complex work, apparently with at least three sections: 'First Isaiah', in 1–39, which contains prophecies of Isaiah from the eighth century BC, much elaborated in the literary tradition of following centuries; 'Second Isaiah', in 40–55, evidently written about 200 years after Isaiah, and referring to Cyrus, the King of Persia, who allowed the Jewish exiles in Babylon to return; and 'Third Isaiah', in 56–66, which seems to come from after the exile. First Isaiah, like his contemporary prophets, has much to say about social injustice in Israel, and about the judgement which Yahweh is bringing on Israel for its injustice and lack of trust. He also emphasizes the holiness of God: see especially the account in chapter 6 of his vision of Yahweh in the Jerusalem

Temple, and of a seraph cleansing his lips with a live coal, so that he can speak the word of Yahweh. Perhaps surprisingly, given his emphasis on God's coming judgement, he often also appeals to God's protection of Mount Zion (i.e. the Temple where he dwells), and prophesies ultimate prosperity for Israel. Such apparent contradictions, however, are not grounds for excluding the favourable prophecies as later additions. King Hezekiah's consultation with Isaiah in II Kings 19 (more or less identical with Isaiah 37) shows that, in the Israelite historical tradition, Isaiah was believed to have given favourable responses at times. We need not believe that he contradicted himself on any particular occasion; rather, the Book of Isaiah's present alternation of judgement and promise prophecies is an aspect of the literary editing of the book (and of course implies a particular view about God's open-ended plans for Israel). Some sections that are more clearly elaborations of the book from after Isaiah's own time are substantial compositions on their own, such as the 'Isaiah Apocalypse' in chapters 24–7, which includes notions such as a universal judgement on the whole earth and a Messianic banquet, which anticipate the details of more strictly apocalyptic books.

Second Isaiah is almost entirely a unified poetic composition, which seems easy to date fairly precisely from its reference to Cyrus. God tells the prophet to

Speak tenderly to Jerusalem / and cry to her / that her warfare is ended, / that her iniquity is pardoned, / that she has received from Yahweh's hand / double for all her sins. (40:2)

Second Isaiah includes four texts which modern scholars have called the 'Servant Songs', and which may refer to the prophet and his role, or more generally to the role of Israel in the world. The fourth song, in 52:13ff., is sometimes taken as evidence for Israelite belief in a 'suffering Messiah', but such a belief is very doubtful. The influence of the song on early Christian thinking about Jesus was to be considerable, but not necessarily straightforward. *Third Isaiah* is partly concerned with correct ritual practice in the (rebuilt) Temple in Jerusalem, but also includes more Messianic sections quoted in the New

Testament, e.g. 61:1ff., which Jesus is shown quoting in the Nazareth synagogue in Luke 4:16ff., with the comment, 'Today this scripture has been fulfilled in your hearing'.

Jeremiah   The prophetic career of Jeremiah can be dated in the last years of the kingdom of Judah, and the Book of Jeremiah adds some information on the fall of Jerusalem and its aftermath to what we learn from II Kings. The book is a mixture of prophecies and sermons, biographical and autobiographical accounts, and laments of Jeremiah, which give us an almost unique insight into personal religion, and into prophetic psychology, in ancient Israel:

Whenever I speak, I cry out, / I shout, 'Violence and destruction!' / For the word of Yahweh has become for me / a reproach and a derision all day long. / If I say, 'I will not mention him, / or speak any more his name', / there is in my heart as it were a burning fire / shut up in my bones, / and I am weary with holding it in, / and I cannot.   (20:8f)

Many sections of the book seem to reflect the language of Deuteronomy, and probably point both to the influence which that book had in the last years of the monarchy, and to some degree of editing of Jeremiah's prophecies by a Deuteronomist. At least one passage of the book has greatly influenced Christian views of the Bible, and led to the belief that a New Testament should follow the Old: 'Behold the days are coming, says Yahweh, when I will make a new covenant with the house of Israel and the house of Judah. . . I will put my law within them, and I will write it upon their hearts; and I will be their God and they shall be my people' (31:31ff.).

Ezekiel   Ezekiel's prophecies, too, can be fairly precisely dated to the earlier part of the exile. They all seem to have been delivered in Babylonia, though with much reference back to events and conditions in Israel, from which Ezekiel had been carried captive in a 'first wave' of exiles in 598 BC. In many respects Ezekiel seems more like a priest than a prophet; and much or all of the book gives the impression of having been written down directly by the prophet, rather than, as with the earlier prophets, delivered orally and then written down by a disciple. Its strongly visionary element begins in the first chapter, traditionally called the 'vision of the chariot', which was to provide both much of the imagery of the Jewish mystical tradition, or Kabbalah, and the image of the four 'living creatures' of Revelation 4, itself to be interpreted later as referring to the writers of the four Gospels in the New Testament. The book includes several allegorical reviews of Israel's history, which are actually the first extensive references to that history in the prophets. They reflect a new Israelite historical consciousness during the exile, which is also evident in the second edition of the Deuteronomistic history, and in the editing of the Pentateuch. Like 'Second Isaiah', the book envisages a restoration of Israel (see the famous 'vision of the valley of dry bones' in 37); and in 40–8 it projects a vision of a restored Temple, in the middle of an ideal Israel reallocated to its tribes. This last, like other parts of Ezekiel, was to influence the apocalyptic tradition; it re-emerges, for example, in the vision of the New Jerusalem in Revelation 21, and also in the account of a restored and purified Temple in Jerusalem in the 'Temple Scroll' from the Dead Sea Scrolls.

The twelve minor prophets   This 'book' comprises 12 smaller collections, the earliest recording the prophecies of Amos, Hosea and Micah from the eighth century BC, and the latest perhaps being Malachi from the fifth century or later. The following are particularly important collections. *Hosea* prophesies disaster for Israel because of its social injustice, with some hope of restoration if the Israelites return to Yahweh. In 1–3 there is a rather complex account of Hosea's marriage to a prostitute, as a symbol of Yahweh's marriage to a faithless Israel. Hosea 6:2: 'After two days he will revive us; / on the third day he will raise us up, / that we may live before him', is probably the main text New Testament writers had in mind in claiming that Jesus' resurrection was 'according to the scriptures'. *Joel* is of uncertain, but probably post-exilic, date; it refers to a locust plague as a harbinger of more apocalyptic disasters to come, but also to an eventual prosperous restoration of Israel and vengeance on its enemies. The verse 2:28f. is a prophecy — 'And it shall come to pass afterward, / that I will pour out my spirit on all flesh' — which was to play an important part in early Christian thinking about Jesus and the movement he launched. *Amos* is slightly earlier than, though from the same general period as, Hosea, and shows similar concerns for social injustice in Israel; it equals Isaiah in the terse vividness of its imagery, and the series of visions in 7–9 especially have been much studied for the light they throw on prophetic psychology. Amos's claim in 14:14–15 that he is 'no prophet, nor a prophet's son' is apparently an attempt to distance himself from any group of 'professional' prophets. *Jonah* has always been one of the most popular books of the Bible, particularly 1–2, the story of Jonah in the stomach of a fish (or 'whale') for three days. The book is about a prophet who refuses Yahweh's command to preach repentance to Nineveh, the Assyrian city; and its satire of this prophet's attitudes may actually be a protest against an excessively exclusive view of Israelite religion. It is most likely to have been written during or after the exile. The story of Jonah coming out of the whale after three days was to influence Christian thinking about the resurrection of Jesus; and in a more general way, too, Jesus' teaching recalled the 'sign' of coming destruction which Jonah was supposed to bring to the Ninevites.

Micah is similar to Amos and Hosea in its attacks on religious and political leaders in the Israel of the eighth century, and in its prophecies of ultimate return to Yahweh and consequent prosperity. The latter theme includes, in 5:2, a promise to Bethlehem (the birthplace of David) that 'from you shall come forth for me / one who is to be ruler in Israel, / whose origin is from of old, / from ancient days' — a Messianic promise which seems to have given rise to the notion that Jesus was not only a descendant of David, but must have been born in Bethlehem. *Haggai* and *Zechariah* clearly come from the time of the Israelite restoration after the exile, and are concerned with the rebuilding of the Jerusalem Temple and the renewal of its cult. They also both refer to one Zerubbabel, of the House of David, and apparently see him (incorrectly, as it turned out) as a Messiah. Zechariah consists mainly of a series of eight visions and their interpretations, and anticipates much of the imagery of Jewish apocalyptic writing. Chapters 9–14 are less closely tied to events and characters of the period immediately following the exile, and probably come from a later time. They include various Messianic references, e.g. 9:9–10, about a king riding to Jerusalem 'on a colt the foal of an ass', and 11:4ff, about a suffering good shepherd, whose wages are weighed out as thirty shekels of silver, which have evidently influenced the Gospel accounts of Jesus' last days. Finally, *Malachi* attacks laxity in Temple worship, idolatry, divorce, and marital infidelity. Chapter 3 promises, or threatens: 'Behold, I send my messenger to prepare the way before me, and the Lord whom you seek will suddenly come to his temple . . .', which in the New Testament is seen as referring both to John the Baptist, and (less explicitly) to Jesus' 'cleansing' of the Temple. The book ends with what seems to be a further identification of this figure: 'Behold, I will send you Elijah the prophet before the great and terrible day of Yahweh comes . . .', which again in the New Testament is referred to John the Baptist.

Psalms In the Jewish tradition this is the first of the 'Writings', or third section of the Hebrew Bible. There are 150 psalms in the book (but details of numbering vary slightly in different Biblical traditions), which are ascribed by headings to different authors or collections, including David; and the book as a whole has traditionally been ascribed to David. According to modern form criticism (discussed below, pp. 98–101), there are several major types of psalms, all of which reflect some kind of cultic situation, in the Jerusalem Temple or elsewhere: the *hymns*, or songs of praise to Yahweh, which include a 'Zion' group praising Yahweh's dwelling in Jerusalem, and an 'enthronement' group claiming his kingship over the world (this latter group has sometimes been associated with a supposed cult of the Israelite kings as divine); *communal laments; royal psalms,* related to various events in kings' lives, such as accession and setting out for battle; the largest group, *individual laments*, which often refer to 'enemies' (who might be personified evil forces) and may also often imply some sort of prophetic reassuring oracle that changes the mood of the lament to confidence; and *individual thanksgiving songs*. In addition, there are some less frequent types of psalms, such as wisdom poems, pilgrimage songs, and communal thanksgivings. Even though the psalms may originally have been closely associated with particular cultic occasions, they have formed the staple of Jewish and Christian prayers, public and private, in all later centuries. Various psalms have greatly influenced the early Christian tradition. In Mark and Matthew Jesus is shown quoting Psalm 22 (in Aramaic) while hanging on his cross, and that psalm and others have contributed many details to the accounts of the crucifixion. Psalm 110: 'Yahweh said to my lord: "Sit at my right hand, / till I make your enemies your footstool" ', was evidently the key text which was thought to 'explain' Jesus' resurrection, and which contributed (along with the vision of 'one like a son of man' coming on the clouds in Daniel 7) to the idea of Jesus' second coming.

Proverbs   This is one of the books called 'wisdom' literature by modern scholars, and like another, Ecclesiastes, it is traditionally attributed to Solomon. The first part of the book, 1–9, is a series of poetic discourses in which a father urges his son to gain wisdom and wisdom itself is personified as a female figure; very likely this personification has been influenced by such ancient Near Eastern goddesses of wisdom as the Egyptian Ma'at. The remainder of the book consists of several collections of mainly two-line proverbs for the successful conduct of life, not all of which have a particular connection with Yahwistic religion. If these terse sayings served the same educational purpose as in other parts of the Near East, then they would have been important in Israelite schools and literary training.

Job   This masterpiece, of mysterious background and uncertain date, is one of the books of the Hebrew Bible that retains a firm hold in modern literary consciousness. It is written in two very different styles: a short folktale-like prologue and epilogue in prose, and the great bulk of the work in verse in between. In the prologue Job is a pious and prosperous man whom God allows Satan to afflict, and in the epilogue God rewards Job's patience with twice what he had before. In the verse, Job curses the day of his birth, and alternates between total despair and a demand to plead his case before Yahweh. His so-called 'comforters', Eliphaz, Bildad, and Zophar, in three series of speeches, question his claims to innocence and urge him to submit to God's providence. This Job refuses to do: 'I hold fast to my righteousness, and will not let it go; / my heart does not reproach me for any of my days' (27:6). A further 'comforter', Elihu, now suddenly appears to answer Job, and many readers have suspected that he is an addition to the original text, intended to correct any unorthodox impressions about divine providence which Job's challenges may have made. If we cut his speeches out, Job's final challenge to God to manifest himself, in 31:35–7, is answered in the most startling fashion in 38ff, where Yahweh speaks to Job 'out of the whirlwind'. 'Where were you when I laid the foundations of the earth? / Tell me, if you have understanding' (38:4). To this Job replies: 'I had heard of you by the hearing of the ear, / but now my eye sees you; / therefore I despise myself, / and repent in dust and ashes' (52:5–6). For some readers this is no answer to the problems posed by the book; for others it is the only possible answer.

The Megilloth   In the Jewish tradition these five fairly short 'scrolls' have become readings for five religious festivals. They appear to be of very various origins. The *Song of Solomon*, or 'Song of Songs', is a series of rather erotic love poems, in which lover and beloved describe alternately their pleasure in each other's bodies; they seem fairly similar to love songs from ancient Egypt. In the Jewish tradition the book has often been allegorized as referring to God's love for Israel and in Christian tradition as referring to Christ's love for the Church or for the individual human soul. *Ruth* is an attractive short story about a woman who persuades Boaz, a relative of her late husband, to marry her. *Lamentations*, traditionally ascribed to Jeremiah, is a series of five laments for Judah and Jerusalem after their devastation by the Babylonians; the first four are alphabetic acrostics. In Christian tradition they have become associated with 'the darkness over the whole land' at Jesus' crucifixion. *Ecclesiastes* is another book of Biblical 'wisdom literature', and is attributed to Solomon. Its general theme 'vanity of vanities! all is vanity', more quietly than Job, questions orthodox assumptions about the meaning of life – and even of 'wisdom'. *Esther* is a partly romantic and partly vengeful tale of how Esther, a beautiful Jewess, married the King of Persia and foiled a plot to have all the Jews in Persia killed.

Daniel   This book is a collection of six stories about Daniel and four visions whose meaning is revealed to him; these revelations have caused the book to be called an 'apocalypse' by modern scholars. Daniel is placed in Babylonia during the Jewish exile, but the historical details seem rather garbled. The visions, and their meanings, clearly point towards the years after 167 BC as the period when the book was actually composed. In that year, the Greek king Antiochus IV of Syria set up the 'abomination that makes desolate' (12:11) in the Jerusalem Temple; but the book encourages loyal Jews to believe that 'his dominion shall be taken away . . . and the kingdom and the dominion . . . shall be given to the people of the saints of the Most High' (7:26f.) in a very short time (Yahwistic worship was in fact restored in the Temple in 164). Daniel has greatly influenced much later Jewish and early Christian thinking: the vision 'with the clouds of heaven there came one like a son of man' in 7:13 seems to have been part of Jesus' expectation of a coming judgement, to have affected his first followers' understanding of Jesus' resurrection and to have led them to expect his second coming. The text of 12:1ff. is the only clear reference in the Hebrew Bible to a general resurrection and judgement of the dead, which was to become a normal part of later Jewish and Christian belief.

Chronicles, Ezra, Nehemiah   These books together form a sort of secondary history from Adam to Ezra, largely parallel to the primary history in the Pentateuch and 'Deuteronomistic History', and apparently drawing mainly (or even entirely) on them, though condensing much of the earlier history into genealogies, and of course giving a unique account of the restoration after the exile. There is some consistency of style and cultic interest in these books, but it is not quite certain that Chronicles and Ezra-Nehemiah were intended to be a single composition. There seems to be confusion in Ezra-Nehemiah about the relative dating of the two men, though less so about their roles: Ezra was to read 'the Law' to the people and enforce it among them, and Nehemiah was to rebuild and repopulate Jerusalem. These are the last historical books of the Hebrew Bible, though Jewish historical work was to revive in Greek in the second century BC with the Books of Maccabees included in the Apocrypha.

The New Testament

The Gospels and the historical Jesus   By almost universal modern consent, Mark was the first of the New Testament Gospels to be written, and it provided the framework, and much of the content, for Matthew and Luke. Because of the similarities between these Gospels produced by this situation, they have traditionally been called the 'Synoptic' Gospels. Some scholars suppose that the author may have drawn on existing written sources about Jesus, such as a collection of parables in Mark 4, the apocalypse in 13, and the account of Jesus' trial and death in 14–15, but this is uncertain. Mark seems to have created the genre of Gospel, but it is less clear what he intended it to be: perhaps an expansion of some basic original preaching about Jesus such as is preserved in the speeches of the Acts of the Apostles or (really only as regards Jesus' death and resurrection) in Paul, but perhaps also an adaptation of the Greek and Roman tradition of biography. However, the arrangement of events in Mark (and the other Gospels) seems to be very casual, and we cannot deduce more than the most basic outline of Jesus' public career from it. Modern form criticism has discerned certain typical and recurring 'forms' in the (originally purely oral) Jesus traditions which the Gospel writers use — legends, miracle stories, exorcisms, and other narratives in the stories about Jesus; and apophthegms (or pronouncement stories), parables, prophetic, apocalyptic and wisdom sayings in the records of Jesus' teaching. Similar forms have been traced, with varying degrees of persuasiveness, in much of the other surviving Jewish and Hellenistic popular literature of Jesus' day, but unfortunately the very popularity of these forms makes it uncertain how much of the authentic Jesus we can now recover from such material. A further difficulty is that the interests and developing theological ideas of the early Christian movement (themselves largely arising from Christian study of the Hebrew Bible) must have greatly affected the way the material was transmitted, especially at its oral stage. Reconstructions of the 'historical Jesus' depend very largely on which data and concepts are taken to be authentic. Nevertheless, with our increasing information, particularly about the Judaism of Jesus' day, and our deepening sociological and psychological awareness of how religious movements can arise, a picture of Jesus seems attainable which is at least plausible and consistent to us. However, we should always remember that any such picture above all reflects our own interests and preconceptions in the twentieth century. The interests and preconceptions of the Gospel writers were of course those of the first century. (See further discussion on these points below, pp. 50–5.)

Mark   The technique of form criticism, mentioned above, has tried to get behind the Gospels to the earlier units of oral tradition about Jesus; a further technique, redaction criticism, has aimed to find out how each Gospel writer has redacted that material, or redacted material from another Gospel, if he is drawing on one, for his own purposes. It seems, from application of this technique, that for Mark, 'the gospel of Jesus Christ, the Son of God' (1:1) began from John the Baptist's appearance and the coming of the Spirit on Jesus as he was baptised. The essence of Jesus' message was: 'The time is fulfilled, and the kingdom of God is at hand' (1:15). Jesus performed exorcisms, and other healings and miracles, which he did not want to be too widely known. He taught further about the kingdom of God in somewhat enigmatic parables. He came into conflict with various other Jewish teachers over the way in which the Jewish law was to be practised. He chose twelve disciples to send out, to extend his teaching and healing, and these disciples, speaking through Peter, eventually recognized him as the Messiah (see Peter's confession at Caesarea Philippi, 8:27–33); but Jesus replied that he had to go to Jerusalem and be killed. He came into Jerusalem in the way predicted for the Messiah in Zechariah 9:9 and 'entered' the Temple, perhaps as Malachi 3:1 predicted. He delivered a final apocalyptic speech (13), predicting the destruction of the Temple and the coming of the Son of Man for judgement (referring to Daniel 7:13ff.). He held a last passover meal with his disciples, which had some overtones of a Messianic banquet. He was tried before the Jewish sanhedrin, or supreme council, confessed to being 'the Messiah, the Son of the Blessed' (14:61), was condemned for blasphemy and then crucified by order of the Roman procurator. A day or so after his burial he was said to have risen and gone back to Galilee, where his disciples would see him. This is of course a highly theological presentation of the Jesus tradition: for Mark, Jesus is quite definitely 'the Messiah' and 'the Son of God' (and even 'the Son of Man'), as the early Christians had come to understand these terms from interpreting various passages in the Hebrew Bible; but Mark also shows Jesus hiding his Messianic status, and saying much about submission and the inevitability of suffering for his followers.

Matthew As we have indicated, most modern scholars believe that this Gospel is based on Mark's. Many further believe that the author has drawn on a hypothetical collection of Jesus' sayings (conventionally called 'Q'), which is also drawn on independently by Luke, but there are certain detailed problems with this view. At all events, Matthew prefaces his Gospel with a genealogy of Jesus, and an account of his birth and infancy in which each event 'took place to fulfil what the Lord had spoken' by various prophets. These 'events' need not be historical in the modern sense of the term, but rather they exemplify the Jewish technique of haggadic midrash, whereby the original prophetic sayings are explained by stories. The author follows Mark's outline more or less faithfully, but he arranges most of Jesus' teaching (including many sayings not in Mark) in five major discourses, which may be meant to recall the 'five books of Moses' which make up the Pentateuch. In many ways this is a highly Jewish work: in Matthew's Sermon on the Mount Jesus says: 'Think not that I have come to abolish the law and the prophets; I have not come to abolish them but to fulfil them' (5:17). However, Jesus is also shown as being very hostile to the Pharisees (see 23, much of which is unique to Matthew). Matthew makes Jesus much less of a hidden Messiah than Mark does, and he adds to Mark's rather low-key report of the resurrection an appearance of Jesus on 'the mountain' in Galilee, at which the disciples are sent to 'make disciples of all nations' (28:10), in what is evidently to be an extensive mission.

Luke Luke's Gospel appears to be based on that of Mark; but it seems intended to be only the first part of the joint work 'Luke-Acts'. As noted above, Luke's relation to Matthew is controversial: the view that both draw independently on a hypothetical sayings-source 'Q' would explain how they add the 'Q' material to Mark in such different ways and places; however, there are detailed objections to the 'Q' hypothesis, and some scholars believe it more likely that Luke drew on both Mark and Matthew. Apart from these sources, Luke includes a great deal of material not in the other synoptics, whose origin is uncertain. Luke begins with a dedication to one 'most excellent Theophilus', which is reminiscent of Greek historical writing of the Hellenistic period, but the rest of the Gospel is far more reminiscent of Old Testament narrative styles (probably known to him through the Septuagint). Luke, like Matthew, has an 'infancy Gospel'. He does not use Matthew's five discourses, but arranges much of the same material into a sort of travel account, from Galilee to Jerusalem. Many readers have noted in this Gospel special emphasis on piety and prayer, on the poor, on women, and on sinners. More controversial is a claim that the author (in Luke–Acts as a whole) divides history into three eras: the time of prophetic preparation in Israel, ending with John the Baptist; Jesus' public life as 'the centre of time'; and the time of the church after his resurrection and ascension – the time of the church being expected to last into an indefinite future. Equally controversial is a claim that this author in effect believes that Jews who do not accept Jesus as the Messiah have ceased to be part of Israel at all.

John   Even in the ancient world this Gospel was called 'the spiritual Gospel', and this title does convey something of its mystical quality. Its general background of thought is very complex: the Gospel almost certainly draws on Jewish traditions of biblical interpretation which also appear in the Aramaic Targums – e.g. the Aramaic *memra*, or 'word', as a periphrasis for God, seems at least partly to explain the 'Word' of the Prologue of John, 1:1ff. (other possibly Targumic elements in John are mentioned below, pp. 109–11). Some elements, too, are similar to esoteric and philosophical trends within the Judaism of its time, and perhaps to such trends in the wider Hellenistic world. Its sources are also complex: sections of the Gospel (including the account of Jesus' trial and death) are more or less parallel to the synoptic Gospels (but not close enough to suggest direct borrowing); there seems to be a 'signs source' from which seven accounts of signs (= miracles) are drawn, to form the starting point of long discourses by Jesus; and similarly certain short sayings of Jesus, comparable to those in the synoptics, form the basis of other discourses. The discourses themselves give the Gospel much of its special quality. Their style has been described as spiral, rather than linear: normal logical progressions and oppositions are bypassed, as the writer keeps circling back to the same themes, of life, light, judgement, the Spirit, the bread of life, water, the Son of Man, and so on. Very often Jesus is shown as opposing, or being opposed by, 'the Jews', or 'the Pharisees': these may be to some extent symbolic opponents (and indeed the names for them shift even within single discourses in the Gospel), but to the extent that they are real the Gospel gives a fairly negative picture of Judaism.

Acts of the Apostles   This book is evidently intended to be the second part of Luke-Acts, in which the resurrected Jesus sends his disciples to be 'my witnesses in Jerusalem and in all Judea and Samaria and to the end of the earth' (1:8) – or at least to the centre of the Roman Empire. As in Luke, there is an opening paragraph reminiscent of the dedications of Greek historical works of the Hellenistic period, along with certain other trappings of Greek historical writing; but again, as in Luke, the work as a whole is more reminiscent of Old Testament narrative styles. There are also elements fairly reminiscent of Greek and Roman novels, but it would be going too far to claim that the basic genre is that of the novel. Its sources are very uncertain. Even in the later passages where the narrator uses 'we' of parts of Paul's travels there is no certainty that an eyewitness is being quoted: this sort of first-person reference has been shown to be a stylistic device in some Hellenistic historical literature. The book falls into two parts: 1–12 deal with the Christian movement in Jerusalem, under Peter's leadership, and its gradual spread beyond Jewish limits; and 13–28 with Paul's missions, mainly to gentiles in Asia Minor and Greece, his arrest in Jerusalem, and his journey as a prisoner to Rome, where he is left 'preaching the kingdom of God and teaching about the Lord Jesus Christ quite openly and unhindered' (30:31) for two years. It is commonly agreed that both of these parts contain some reliable traditions about the earliest church and its beliefs; but it is hard to reconcile the account given of Paul's activities with what Paul himself says in his letters, and even harder to find the peculiarities of Paul's theology in the missionary speeches he makes in Acts: many scholars conclude that Luke is giving a rather garbled version of Paul's activities and putting typical missionary speeches in his mouth, from no real knowledge of his epistles or theology.

The Epistles of Paul Manuscripts of the New Testament include thirteen epistles of Paul. Nearly all modern scholars agree that seven of these were written by Paul, in the 50s AD, in roughly the order: I Thessalonians, Galatians, I and II Corinthians, Philippians, Philemon, Romans (though II Corinthians and Philippians especially seem to have been assembled from several originally separate letters). Many scholars argue that some or all of the others (II Thessalonians, Colossians, Ephesians, I and II Timothy, Titus) were written by followers or imitators of Paul, to develop aspects of his thought to meet new conditions after his death.

I Thessalonians is a general letter expressing Paul's delight at the spread of the Christian movement in Thessalonica. Perhaps its most interesting passage is 4:13ff., which shows how vividly Paul expected 'the Lord' to 'descend from heaven' in the near future, when 'the dead in Christ will rise first; then we who are alive, who are left, shall be caught up together with them in the clouds to meet the Lord in the air'. This expectation seems to owe something to the vision of 'one like a son of man' in Daniel 7. *Galatians* first raises one of the major problems of Paul's mission and thinking: whether gentile Christians should be circumcised and have to keep the Jewish food laws, as some Jewish Christians in Galatia were claiming. Paul first relates his own contacts with the original Jewish Christians in Jerusalem, which had confirmed that he had been entrusted with preaching to the gentiles; he then develops an argument, by way of a midrashic interpretation of passages from the Hebrew Bible — 'Christ redeemed us from the curse of the law, having become a curse for us' (3:13), and that 'Abraham "believed God, and it was reckoned to him as righteousness" ' (3:6, quoting Genesis 15:6) long before the law was given to the Israelites — that the gentiles are thus 'free of the law. (See below, pp. 81–2 on 'midrash').

I Corinthians gives a fascinating picture of a Christian community in a major Greek city, and has recently been much quarried by sociologists of early Christianity. The community was a factious one, prone to enthusiasm based on claims to esoteric religious knowledge and liable to disregard normal sexual conventions. Paul attempts to discipline their enthusiasm by recalling 'Christ crucified, a stumbling block to the Jews and folly to the Gentiles' (1:23); by restricting sexual activity to marriage and advocating celibacy if possible 'in view of the present distress' (7:26); by trying to regulate their conduct of the 'Lord's supper' along less factious lines; by subordinating their various 'spiritual gifts' to the good of the whole community and by presenting the resurrection as something lying ahead for the whole group, not something that individuals can anticipate now. *II Corinthians* seems to be an assemblage from several originally independent letters, and its parts to come from different stages of a prolonged controversy. Paul defends himself against agitators from outside Corinth, who proved their spiritual powers by working miracles and by showy eloquence. He again recalls that 'while we live we are always being given up to death for Jesus' sake, so that the life of Jesus may be manifested in our mortal flesh' (4:11); but in 11–12 he tries 'boasting' himself, giving a remarkable picture of his own religious experiences.

Romans has often been taken as the key text for Paul's thought as a whole. In 1–8 he argues that the coming of Jesus as the Messiah has made it possible for both gentiles and Jews to be 'justified' before God. Gentiles have failed to heed the truth about God which God has shown to them, and Jews have equally failed to live up to the law and the promises revealed to them. But now, both can accept the 'redemption which is in Christ Jesus, whom God put forward as an expiation by his blood, to be received by faith' (3:24f.). The section 9–11 has often been considered an argument about predestination, but more specifically it aims to show, again by a midrashic exposition of texts from the Hebrew Bible, that God has 'hardened the heart' of the majority of Jews, so that the gentiles may have a chance to be 'grafted in their place' in God's scheme of salvation; but Paul fully expects that in time 'these natural branches will be grafted back into their own olive tree' (11:24). Paul's perspective on the relations of Jews and Christians, in many ways the central problem in his thought, is much more ecumenical than those in Luke and John. Like other aspects of his thought, this perspective is modified in the letters supposed to be by Paul's followers and imitators, but *Ephesians* sums it up memorably: 'For [Christ] is our peace, who has made us both one, and has broken down the dividing wall of hostility, by abolishing in his flesh the law of commandments and ordinances, that he might create in himself one new man in place of the two . . .' (2:14f.).

Hebrews   This epistle (or better 'sermon', or even 'treatise') has come to be grouped with the epistles of Paul, but it is in fact anonymous, and the circumstances of its writing are unclear. By way of a typological interpretation of passages from the Hebrew Bible it argues that Christ is a final revelation of God, superior to any other, and that his sacrifice of himself supersedes the Jewish sacrifices. For example, the mysterious priest-king Melchizedek, to whom Abraham gives a tithe in Genesis 14, in Hebrews becomes a type of the 'high priest' Christ, by implication higher than the priests of the Jewish Temple. This sort of exegesis of the Hebrew Bible was to become very common in the Christian tradition, as will be shown below, pp. 86–9.

The Catholic Epistles   These seven 'catholic' or 'general' epistles are attributed to the apostles James, Peter, John and Jude, but the attributions are very questionable, and all of the letters seem later than the time of these apostles. *James* gives much ethical instruction of a traditional Jewish kind, and has sometimes been taken to contradict Paul's teaching on 'justification by faith' rather than 'works'. It also owes much to the wisdom tradition of the Hebrew Bible. *I Peter* aims to encourage Christian communities in Asia Minor who are undergoing persecution, with a mixture of wisdom and apocalyptic material, ethical instruction, and what seem to be fragments of Christian hymns. *I John* seems to come from the same circle as the Gospel of John, and apparently aims to reject gnostic understandings of Jesus which had appeared in that circle (and which the Gospel may even have inspired).

Revelation   This last book of the Bible is a series of revelations to one 'John', exiled to the island of Patmos, who is traditionally identified with the author of the Gospel, but in fact the two works are very different in style and in outlook. Like other apocalypses in the Jewish/Christian tradition, it encourages those undergoing persecution to stand firm, by presenting a series of visions supposed to indicate God's plan for the world. John begins with letters to seven churches in Asia (themselves of a rather visionary kind); then presents three cycles of visions (of seven seals, of seven trumpets, and of seven bowls), with intervening and following visions of God in his heavenly court, of earthly powers (presumably Rome in particular) represented by beasts which are cast down, of the Lamb which was slain, of the loosing of Satan for a final conflict, and of 'the holy city, the new Jerusalem, coming down out of heaven from God, prepared as a bride adorned for husband' (21:2). The imaginative power of this book has never been doubted, or the extensive influence of its symbolism in later times. Much of that symbolism goes back, by way of the Jewish apocalyptic tradition, to the earliest stages of ancient Near Eastern religious literature, accounting, perhaps, for the truly awesome quality of this conclusion to the Bible.

Chapter 3

Leading themes of the Bible

In this chapter, ten biblical themes or clusters of ideas are presented. They are central themes, and therefore a convenient entry into the Bible's world of thought; they have all been shown to have a background in the general culture of the ancient Near East and they all reflect the process of continual reinterpretation from one book of the Bible to another, which has been one of the central concerns of this book. Given our uncertainties about when and how parts of the Bible came to be written, and given the Bible's complex internal cross-references and allusions, any such presentation will be somewhat arbitrary, and disputable on many points. Only a few such points will be discussed here, and then only when some widely held opinion seems to obscure the essential continuity of the biblical tradition. The section on promise, threat and fulfilment, pp. 50–5, includes an attempt to clarify a common confusion between the apocalyptic tradition, which may have influenced Jesus (and which certainly influenced the biblical tradition about him), and the question of his outlook, or consciousness. A comparison of Spirits on pp. 74–9 a sort of appendix to this chapter, is an attempt to compare at some length a text from the Hebrew Bible with one on a similar theme from the New Testament, as an example of both continuity and transformation in the biblical tradition.

God

God is in many ways the leading character of the Bible, and the Bible presents human history as being under his ultimate control. Most Jews and Christians over the centuries have felt no need to question the existence or nature of this 'character', but, with modern critical study of the Bible and its cultural

43

background, and modern insight into the ways religions emerge and develop, such questions naturally arise. The Bible itself claims that God revealed himself progressively to Adam, to Noah, to Abraham, to Moses, to David, to the prophets, and so on; and the New Testament claims that he has finally revealed himself in Jesus the Messiah. Such claims, we can now see, have many parallels in other religions. What perhaps distinguishes the biblical claims is that the revelations are arranged in this progressive sequence, but then of course the sequence itself is a literary device – an aspect of the way in which the texts have been arranged within the Bible.

The word 'God' is normally used to translate the Hebrew 'El', or its plural form 'Elohim' (the plural does not necessarily indicate that God was once thought to be many). This word is far from being unique to Israelite religion: it is the general term in Semitic languages for a god, as well as for a particular god 'El' in Canaanite religion; and it is the word also used for 'other gods' throughout the Bible itself. The particular name for the God of Israel is 'Yhwh' (or some close variant), normally today vocalized as 'Yahweh'. Jews have traditionally avoided pronouncing this name, and substituted 'Adonai' ('the Lord') whenever it occurs, a practice followed by most English translations of the Bible. As we have seen in chapter 1, p. 10, the Bible has variant accounts of when this name began to be used: the best known story is that it was revealed to Moses at Sinai (or Horeb, Exodus 3). The use of the name does not necessarily imply a strict monotheism – in fact much of the Hebrew Bible clearly implies the existence of other gods, as when Joshua says 'choose this day whom you will serve, whether the gods your fathers served in the region beyond the River, or the gods of the Amorites in whose land you dwell; but as for me and my house, we will serve Yahweh' (Joshua 24:15), a passage which seems to admit in advance that many Israelites *would* be tempted to serve such other gods. The biblical prophets, of course, stand for Yahweh, but the first of them to attack other gods as being literally nothing but man–made idols is 'Second Isaiah', writing at the end of the Babylonian exile.

In the post-exilic literature, and in the New Testament, there is scarcely any question raised about the oneness of God. Jesus, in Mark 12:29f., is shown quoting the famous *Shema* of Deuteronomy 6:4: 'The first [commandment] is, "Hear, O Israel: the Lord our God, the Lord is one; and you shall love the Lord your God with all your heart, and with all your soul, and with all your mind, and with all your strength" '. Paul's graphic account of the supposed degeneration of Greek gentile culture in Romans 1 suggests that 'what can be known about God is plain to [the gentiles] because God has shown it to them . . . [but] claiming to be wise they became fools, and exchanged the glory of the immortal God for images resembling mortal man or birds or animals or reptiles' (1:19–23 – a clear allusion, incidentally, to the creation account in Genesis 1, discussed below). According to the Bible, then, adherence to Yahwism involves a sort of practical monotheism (or henotheism, as it is sometimes called) from an early date in the history of Israel; but strict monotheism only emerges in the later literature – perhaps as a conclusion which the Bible's editors during the exile drew from their work on the older traditions.

The imagery used of God in the Bible is predominantly drawn from human beings and human society, but to some extent also from the natural world. In the Hebrew Bible God is very frequently a king, or a judge, or a shepherd, or some other sort of ruler. He is also sometimes a rather stern father, as in Psalm 103:13: 'As a father pities his children, / so Yahweh pities those who fear him'. In the New Testament references to God as a loving father are noticeably more frequent, with Jesus shown addressing him as such. It has also been suggested (though this is not quite certain) that the Aramaic term 'Abba', preserved in a few passages of the New Testament, indicates some kind of uniquely intimate sense of relationship between God and Jesus or Jesus' followers. There is a certain amount of feminine imagery for God in the Bible, e.g. womb, breast, conception, giving birth, nurturing, etc.; but whether such imagery indicates a survival of earlier matriarchal traits amid a general biblical trend to patriarchalize God is more than the nature of our sources will let us know. Cosmic imagery for God drawn from the natural world is very noticeable, e.g., in the Psalms, and in such examples of 'speculative wisdom' as God's reply to Job in Job 38ff. Almost all the types of biblical imagery for God have parallels elsewhere in the ancient Near East.

Creation

The Bible contains two explicit accounts of God's creation of the world, in Genesis 1–2, but many other partial accounts and allusions as well. The accounts in Genesis 1–2 have often been attributed respectively to the 'P' and 'J' 'sources' of the Pentateuch. Both accounts have overtones of other, more mythological creation stories from the Near East. The Hebrew word *tehom* in 1:2, usually translated as 'the deep', may be an allusion to Tiamat, the dragon of chaos who is overcome in battle by Marduk in the Babylonian New Year creation story *Enuma Elish*; and the setting of a 'firmament' to separate the waters 'above' and 'below', with lights in the firmament to 'rule' the day and the night, seems to be drawn from the same tradition of myths. The first account is structured on the seven days of the week (a unit of time the Israelites are the earliest people known to have used) and ends with God resting on and 'hallowing' the seventh day, or Sabbath. On the sixth day 'God created man in his own image, in the image of God he created him; male and female he created them' (1:27), the 'image' here perhaps referring especially to the authority which God then gives man over the rest of his creation. In the second account God first moistened the dry earth, then 'formed man of dust from the ground, and breathed into his nostrils the breath of life; and man became a living being' (2:7). Later, God 'took the man and put him in the garden of Eden to till it and keep it' (2:15), allowed man to give names to every living creature, and finally made woman from one of his ribs. The notion that man tills the earth on God's behalf is perhaps closer to general ancient Mesopotamian ideas than the claim in the first account that man has 'dominion' over the other creatures.

Genesis 1–2 give accounts of God's creation in which mythological elements have been somewhat disguised. The many other allusions to creation in the Hebrew Bible are mxinly in poetic contexts, and draw more freely on mythical motifs. Psalm 29, beginning 'Ascribe to Yahweh, O sons of gods, / ascribe to Yahweh glory and strength', then claiming that 'the voice of Yahweh is upon the waters', and finally that 'Yahweh sits enthroned over the flood; / Yahweh sits enthroned as king for ever', is almost indistinguishable in its imagery from surviving Canaanite religious poetry. Psalm 104 has often been compared to the 'Hymn to the Sun' by the celebrated 'heretic' Egyptian Pharaoh Akhenaton. 'Second Isaiah', in 51:9ff., first addresses God as creator: 'Was it not you that cut Rahab in pieces, / that pierced the dragon? / Was it not you that dried up the sea, / the waters of the great deep?', then alludes to God also 'making the depths of the sea a way / for the redeemed to pass over', at the Israelites' exodus from Egypt, and finally announces that similarly the 'ransomed of Yahweh' will soon be able to return to Jerusalem – a transition from the mythical to the historical, as it were. The wisdom literature includes speculation about God's means of creation. Proverbs 8:22ff. is a hymn spoken by the personified Wisdom about her role as a 'master workman' for God at the creation: 'When he established the heavens, I was there . . .'; and similar ideas appear in Job 28.

The early Christians soon came to identify Christ with Wisdom, God's agent of creation in such texts. What may be an early Christian hymn appears in Colossians 1:15–20: '[Christ] is the image of the invisible God, the first born of all creation; for in him all things were created . . .' A further development of this identification can be seen in the Prologue to John 1:1–18: 'He was in the beginning with God; all things were made through him, and without him was not anything made which was made'. Paul evidently sees Christ as the agent of a 'new creation' of the world: 'the creation itself will be set free from its bondage to decay and obtain the glorious liberty of the children of God' (Romans 8:21). Finally, Revelation, after recounting visions which owe a good deal to early Near

Eastern creation accounts, concludes: 'Then I saw a new heaven and new earth; for the first heaven and the first earth has passed away, and the sea was no more . . .' (21:1ff.).

Covenant

The biblical notion of covenant is closely associated with the theme of a progressive revelation of God: God is shown making covenants with Noah, with Abraham, with the Israelites at Sinai under Moses, with David, and so on. Covenants were a normal part of the political life of the ancient Near East, and very likely the biblical notion of covenant is based on such practice. If this is so, however, notions of God's exclusive covenant with Israel may only have entered the biblical tradition at a comparatively late stage — perhaps in the late monarchy, as a reaction to Israel's disappointing experience of international political covenants. More precisely, such notions may first have appeared in Deuteronomy, in the seventh century BC, and from there been used as a way of interpreting and ordering a variety of earlier, perhaps still oral, traditions. In other words, covenant, like the idea of a series of self-revelations by God discussed above, seems more of a biblical literary device than it is a reflection of a central concept of Israelite cult during the monarchic period. It is noteworthy that it is *not* a central concept in the early prophetic literature, the only real exception to this being a reference to an unspecified covenant in Hosea 8:1ff.

The covenants which the Bible describes God as making with men are actually of two different types: the unconditional and the conditional. In the first, as with Abraham (Genesis 15) and with David (II Samuel 7), God promises absolutely: 'To your descendants I give this land, from the river of Egypt to the great river, the river Euphrates . . .' (Genesis 15:18; these very wide boundaries for Israel were, incidentally, never realized) and 'your house and your kingdom shall be made sure for ever before me: your throne shall be established for ever' (II Samuel 7:16). It has been suggested that the covenant with Abraham is based on grants of lands as fiefs to loyal servants of the king in the ancient Near East; and that the covenant with David is similar to other dynastic oracles of the period.

The conditional covenant is above all represented in the Bible by the Sinai covenant. The most convincing political parallels suggested for this are Hittite treaties of the fourteenth and thirteenth centuries BC between a greater and a lesser king (or vassal). In such treaties, the great king names himself and his titles, lists the benefits he has already conferred on the vassal, gives various stipulations which the vassal must observe, calls gods to witness the treaty, and lists blessings which will follow from observing it and curses which will follow from not doing so. These are, more or less, the elements of the Sinai covenant as given in Exodus 19–24 and in various parts of Deuteronomy (though 'heaven and earth' are called to witness the treaty in Deuteronomy, rather than gods). Such covenants, of course, are intended to exclude any other alliances and loyalties on the part of the vassal. The biblical adaptation of the covenant form, however, includes some unusual features. Most of the legal material of the Pentateuch has been included under the stipulations of the Sinai covenant, which gives that material a sort of blanket divine authentication which is unique in the ancient world. Another unusual feature of the Sinai covenant is the emotive language that can describe it, especially in Deuteronomy: 'And because you hearken to these ordinances, and keep and do them, Yahweh your God will keep with you the covenant and the steadfast love which he swore to your father to keep' (7:12; the Hebrew term *hesed*, usually rendered by the RSV, as here, as 'steadfast love', and by the AV as 'loving kindness', is a highly distinctive aspect of the Hebrew Bible's characterization of God).

It is often said that the Israelite prophets appealed to the stipulations of the Sinai covenant in their calls for social justice in Israel. However, as we have seen, the earlier prophets do not, in fact, regularly refer to a covenant, and it is safest to assume that they based their appeals on more general considerations of what was appropriate for Yahweh's community. Once the notion *was* established as a central religious concept, the later prophets did often appeal to it. Thus Jeremiah claims both that God's original covenant has been broken by Israel, and that 'Behold the days are coming, says Yahweh, when I will make a new covenant with the house of Israel and the house of Judah, not like the covenant which I made with their fathers when I took them by the hand to bring them out of the land of Egypt . . . I will put my law within them, and I will write it upon their hearts; and I will be their God, and they shall be my people' (31:31ff.). This might be a rather interesting case of a concept that began as a biblical literary device influencing the ongoing oral tradition of prophecy.

Jesus in the Gospels makes little reference to the covenant, but the earliest tradition we have about his Last Supper (I Corinthians 11:23ff.) has him saying, 'This cup is the new covenant in my blood . . .' (evidently comparing himself to the 'old' covenant sacrifice in Exodus 24:3ff.). Similarly Paul believes that God 'has made us competent to be ministers of a new covenant, not in a written code but in the Spirit' (II Corinthians 3:6). Hebrews explicitly quotes Jeremiah 31:31ff. at 8:8ff., and develops rather elaborately the typology of old and new covenants, a typology which eventually led to the Christian scriptures being called the 'New Testament'.

Promise, threat, and fulfilment

A great many texts of the Bible are eschatological, i.e. they point forward from the occasion when they are supposed to have been spoken or written to some future fulfilment; and many texts, especially in the New Testament, refer explicitly or implicitly to the fulfilment of texts from the Hebrew Bible. The difference between the two Testaments in this respect should not be exaggerated. It would be misleading to claim that the Hebrew Bible is exclusively forward looking — because many periods of history that it records, as well as many individual events, are presented as fulfilments of earlier promises and threats — and equally misleading to say that the New Testament is backward looking, because it in fact refers to many expectations which are still to be fulfilled. Eschatology is not unique to biblical religious literature, but that literature seems more consistently eschatological than any other in the ancient Near East.

At the very beginning of Israelite history, God promises Abraham, 'Go from your country and your kindred and your father's house to the land that I will show you. And I will make of you a great nation' (Genesis 12:1f.). Later he promises Moses that he will bring his people out of Egypt 'to a good and broad land, a land flowing with milk and honey' (Exodus 3:8). Joshua's conquest of the land of Palestine is presented by the Deuteronomistic historian as fulfilling these promises: 'Thus Yahweh gave to Israel all the land which he swore to give to their fathers; and having taken possession of it they settled there' (Joshua 21:43). After the disturbed period of the 'Judges' and of Saul, God makes further promises to David: 'When your days are fulfilled and you lie down with your fathers, I will raise up your offspring after you . . . and I will establish the throne of his kingdom for ever' (2 Samuel 7:12f.).

However, even during the reign of David, God is shown warning the king through prophets of the consequences of his less moral actions; and during the later monarchy the prophets, or at least the prophets of Yahweh, become increasingly grim in their predictions of disaster for Israel and its rulers. The earliest of the prophets whose oracles gave rise to a separate book in the Bible, Amos, threatens that Israel has no further good to expect from God: 'Woe to you who desire the day of Yahweh! / Why would you have the day of Yahweh? / It is darkness and not light' (5:18); and this becomes almost the prevailing view of these prophets down to the final collapse of the monarchy. At the same time, however, these same prophets often speak of a quite visionary prosperity as about to come: 'The people who walked in darkness have seen a great light . . . For to us a child is born, / to us a son is given; / and the government will be upon his shoulder' (Isaiah 9:2ff., evidently referring to the accession of a new king in Jerusalem, perhaps Hezekiah). Nevertheless, the overall biblical judgement on the monarchy, as enshrined in the Deuteronomistic account of its last days, was to be negative.

The experience of exile prompted much reflection on the

meaning of Israel's history. The Book of Ezekiel includes several very negative reviews of that history in both symbolic and literal forms; for example, chapter 16 presents Jerusalem as a bastard orphan who was adopted by Yahweh and brought up delicately to be his wife, but became a prostitute whose lovers will very shortly turn against her. Chapter 20 gives a more literal account of Israel's history from the time of the exodus from Egypt, in language reminiscent of the Deuteronomistic History (which may indeed have been finally edited at about the same time). However, Ezekiel is confident that God will eventually 'take the people of Israel from the nations among which they have gone, and will gather them from all sides, and bring them to their own land'; further, 'David my servant shall be their prince for ever. I will make a covenant of peace with them; it shall be an everlasting covenant with them . . . Then the nations will know that I Yahweh sanctify Israel, when my sanctuary is in the midst of them for evermore' (37:21ff.). In 40–8 he gives a visionary account of this expected restoration of the land, of Jerusalem, and of the Temple. Later in the exile, 'Second Isaiah' made a more specific promise of a return to Israel as the result of Cyrus' capture of Babylon and this indeed followed shortly thereafter.

The return from exile is presented by Ezra and Nehemiah as a fulfilment of Jeremiah's promise of a return after seventy years. However, even in the account of the rebuilding of the Temple there is a note of disappointment: 'But many of the priests and Levites and heads of fathers' houses, old men who had seen the first house, wept with a loud voice when they saw this foundation being laid . . .' (Ezra 3:12). The prophets Haggai and Zechariah clearly expect Zerubbabel, a descendant of the house of David, to become king, but the imperial policies of Persia would hardly have allowed this. What seem to be the last of the Hebrew Bible's prophets, 'Second Zechariah' (i.e. Zechariah 9–14), and Malachi, reflect rather vague and visionary hopes for the future, as well as a transition from prophetic to apocalyptic language (both works were to be much drawn on in the New Testament).

Biblical apocalyptic is in many ways a direct development

om Israelite prophecy, but it reflects the new political condi-
ons of Israel as a subject people after the exile, and really
ily emerged as an independent genre after all immediate hopes
: political restoration had faded. The apocalyptic writers no
nger see foreign powers as God's agents in punishing Israel
or its unfaithfulness, but as evil and completely opposed to
;od; and consequently they no longer see God as being in im-
nediate control of events in the world. Their writings consist
irgely of revelations, in visionary and allegorical form, of
istory down to the writer's time, and of events expected in
he immediate future. These include persecutions of Israel, a
decisive intervention of God in favour of Israel, God's judgement against the foreign powers and other sinners, and his
re-establishment of a final, righteous kingdom of Israel. Daniel
is the only strictly apocalyptic book in the Hebrew Bible (and
even in Daniel really only 7–12). However, a number of others
appear in 'intertestamental' literature, including the Dead Sea
Scrolls.

Most of the books of the New Testament, including the
Gospels, reflect elements of the apocalyptic tradition. Especially since the later nineteenth century it has often been
claimed, from the evidence of the Synoptic Gospels, that Jesus'
outlook was a consistently apocalyptic one: he announced that
the 'kingdom of God' was at hand and saw his own teaching
and actions as signs of its 'breaking in'; he referred to biblical
texts as being fulfilled in his life; he taught much, especially
in his parables, about the paradoxical and unexpected nature
of the 'kingdom'; he may have delivered an apocalyptic
discourse (Mark 13 and parallels); and he may have seen his
death in particular as the start of the new covenant. This supposed apocalyptic outlook is then used as the criterion for
distinguishing authentic and inauthentic elements in the tradition about him. Such arguments proceed from the known
characteristics of the literary form apocalypse and the fact that
some of these characteristics appear in the traditions about
Jesus, to the conclusion that Jesus' essential consciousness was
an apocalyptic one, which is surely illegitimate. We can say
very little for certain about Jesus' education or precise cultural

formation, but it must surely have included a much wider range
of biblical traditions than merely the rather recondite and
bookish apocalyptic one. Recent scholarship has begun to pay
attention to various *non*-apocalyptic elements in the Synoptic
tradition about Jesus' teaching: quite extensive wisdom and
general ethical elements, and interest in the correct interpretation of the Bible. We should not reject these elements as inauthentic just because they are not exclusively apocalyptic. We
should also not automatically reject John's Gospel as an inauthentic tradition about Jesus just because it is less apocalyptic
than the Synoptics (or should we say because it uses apocalyptic in a more 'interpreted' way than they do?). We should not
argue from a supposed apocalyptic outlook to what Jesus could
and could not have expected to happen in the future. Although
he is shown telling his disciples, 'Go nowhere among the
Gentiles . . . but go rather to the lost sheep of the house of
Israel' (Matthew 10:5f.), he might very well have expected 'the
nations' eventually to 'run to' Israel, as such non-apocalyptic
elements of the prophetic tradition as Isaiah 55:5 anticipated.
Above all, we should be very careful about exactly what interpretative techniques we are using in claiming to get behind the
text of the Gospels.

There is, however, to repeat, no doubt that the early Christian tradition in the New Testament often interprets Jesus, and
the movement which he gave rise to, in apocalyptic categories;
Paul's Epistles, for example, are dominated by them. He writes,
'From now on, therefore, we regard no one from a human point
of view; even though we once regarded Christ from a human
point of view, we regard him thus no longer. Therefore, if anyone
is in Christ, he is a new creation; the old is passed away, behold
the new has come' (II Corinthians 5:16f.). In I Thessalonians
4:13ff. he seems to believe quite literally that 'the Lord' will descend from heaven during Paul's own lifetime: 'then we who are
alive, who are left, shall be caught up together with [the dead]
in the clouds to meet the Lord in the air'. However, he can also
warn: 'Therefore do not pronounce judgement before the time,
before the Lord comes, who will bring to light the things now
hidden in darkness' (I Corinthians 4:5). Clearly, apocalyptic

images once used of God's 'coming' have been transferred to Christ. We are not quite certain how or why this happened, but we can see from the New Testament that the early Christians' belief in Jesus' appearances after his death (for which our earliest source is I Corinthians 15) was expressed in the terms of such texts as Psalm 110 ('Yahweh said to my lord: "Sit at my right hand, / till I make your enemies your footstool" ') and Daniel 7. Despite these expectations for the future, Paul also clearly believes that Christians are already 'in Christ', or 'in the Lord'.

Law and righteousness

Covenants in the ancient Near East often involved detailed stipulations; and in the Bible God's covenants with Israel involve legal expectations − in fact all the extensive legal sections of the Pentateuch are presented as spoken or to be spoken by Moses to the people of Israel in connection with the covenant at Sinai. If we conclude that the notion of God's covenant is a late development in Israelite thinking, then we will probably also believe that these legal sections in fact come from different periods and reflect Israelite cultural development over many centuries. Archaeologists have now recovered several extensive ancient Mesopotamian law codes, which show many parallels, both formal and material, to the Pentateuch legal texts. Interestingly enough, however, these other codes purport to be compiled by kings and offered by them to gods, perhaps as testimonies of their righteousness (e.g. the Code of Hammurabi of Babylon actually shows the king offering his laws to Shamash, the Sun God and protector of justice), whereas the Pentateuch texts are conveyed by Moses from God to the people. In both cases there is some doubt how far the codes were real laws, intended to be applied in courts. In Babylonia, none of the numerous surviving court records quotes any code. In the Bible, Deuteronomy 16:18ff. speaks of the appointment of 'judges and officers in all your towns', and later of some sort of appellate court in Jerusalem, but nothing of what law they are to apply. The actual trials referred to in the Bible seem to be conducted before 'elders' sitting 'in the gate', according to general traditions of equity, and frequently resorting to oracles or ordeals. The Israelite kings are not said to have enforced any particular legal code, at least until the discovery of the 'book of the law' during Temple repairs under Josiah (II Kings 22; the book in question, as suggested elsewhere, may be more or less identical with Deuteronomy). The Pentateuch laws therefore seem to be somewhat 'ideal' literary creations, from late in the monarchy and after, though of course reflecting, some much older legal ideas.

There is no doubt, however, that during and after the exile these laws played a vital part in keeping Israelite culture alive. In Nehemiah 8f. Ezra is shown reading the 'book of the law of Moses' to the returned Israelites in Jerusalem; then the 'heads of the fathers' houses of all the people, with the priests and the Levites' come to study the law relating to the 'feast of booths', or Sukkoth (this is an archetypal picture of the Jewish 'house of study' throughout the ages); Ezra confesses the Israelites' previous disregard of the law; and finally the people as a whole 'make a firm covenant' to observe the law. Whatever the exact date of Ezra, and whatever form the 'law of Moses' had reached by then, this account establishes that law as the future basis of Jewish life. The final editing of the Pentateuch, with alternating law and narrative, but all supposedly written down by Moses, places the law firmly within God's constitutive and unquestionable revelation.

Nevertheless, that law could hardly be final. During the Persian and especially the Hellenistic periods Judaism was exposed to many new cultural pressures. The Books of Maccabees, among the Apocrypha, make it clear that many even of the Jewish leaders in the second century BC were eager to adapt their way of life to the highly prestigious Greek customs. The Maccabees led a revolt to defend Jewish culture; and perhaps a little later the Pharisees emerged as a conservative movement within Judiasm. Much is obscure about the Pharisees, but it is at least clear that they accepted (some would say invented) the 'oral' as well as the written law, i.e. an authoritative 'oral tradition' of correct interpretation, which, like the written law, they traced back through Ezra to Moses.

Jesus' attitude to the Jewish law has been much debated. In the Gospels he is regularly shown in conflict with the 'scribes' and/or 'Pharisees', e.g. about his disciples plucking grains of wheat to eat on the Sabbath, about whether he must be in league with diabolical powers if he can perform exorcisms, about performing healings on the Sabbath, about whether the Pharisees' oral law was really anything more than the 'traditions of men' and about his association with 'sinners' such as tax-collectors and prostitutes. None of these conflicts implies any direct criticism of the law itself, or at least of the written law. In Matthew especially Jesus is portrayed as a legal teacher himself. In the 'Sermon on the Mount' (Matthew 5–7) Jesus says, 'Think not that I have come to abolish the law and the prophets; I have not come to abolish them but to fulfil them. For truly, I say to you, till heaven and earth pass away, not an iota, not a dot, will pass from the law until all is accomplished' (5:17f.). In the following antithesis, 'You have heard that it was said . . . but I say to you . . .', Jesus is hardly attacking the law, or even trying to rewrite it, but he does seem to imply that the law has been understood in a somewhat lax manner, which he wishes to correct. Jesus may possibly here be teaching a 'law of the kingdom', such as some Jews expected to be given in the last days, though there are not in fact many clearly eschatological features about these antitheses.

Paul claimed to have been 'a Hebrew born of Hebrews; as to the law a Pharisee, as to zeal a persecutor of the Church, as to righteousness under the law blameless' (Philippians 3:5f.). Especially since the Reformation it has often been argued, mainly on the basis of Romans, that Paul had become personally disillusioned with the law: 'I was once alive apart from the law, but when the commandment came, sin revived and I died; the very commandment which promised life proved to be death to me' (Romans 7:9f.); and that, with Paul's 'conversion' to Christianity, he came to reject totally the law as a means to achieve righteousness (or to justify oneself) before God. This argument should be treated with caution. Paul never speaks in his own letters of being converted to Christianity, but only says that 'he who set me apart before I was born, and had called me through his grace, was pleased to reveal his Son to [or 'in'] me, in order that I might preach him among the gentiles' (Galatians 1:15f.). Having then accepted Jesus as the Messiah, he was very quickly faced with the problem of whether the gentiles he preached to should have to practise the law, and a large part of Paul's thinking is concerned to explain why they should not. The overall argument of Romans 1–8 is that all men, Jews and gentiles, have 'fallen short' of what God required of them, but that all can be 'justified' by accepting Jesus as the Messiah. Paul seems clear that there is nothing wrong with the law or with Judaism, only with Jews who find a false security before God in the law. He is equally clear that gentiles should be free of the law, because it was given only to Israel. It is *not* very clear from Romans whether he thinks Jews who *have* accepted Jesus as the Messiah should have to go on keeping the law. Probably he takes it that the Jews as a whole have *not* accepted Jesus (though Romans 9–11 argues that they will do so when God ceases to 'harden their hearts'), and so the question does not yet arise.

Sacrifice and expiation

Instructions on sacrifices to be performed by the Israelites, on ordinary and extraordinary occasions, take up much of the legal sections of the Pentateuch. Most of these sacrifices are shown as being started immediately during the Israelites' period in the wilderness, at the 'tent of meeting' which accompanied their wanderings. This tent is a perhaps fictional anticipation of the Jerusalem Temple; like the form of that Temple, the details of sacrifice seem to have been largely taken over by the Israelites in Palestine from their predecessors and neighbours, along with so much else of their cult. There are traces in the Bible of a view of sacrifices as the food of God (see Leviticus 21:6), which is how they were commonly regarded in the ancient world. In Genesis 8, Noah, as soon as the flood has receded, 'took of every clean animal and of every clean bird, and offered burnt offerings on the altar. And when Yahweh smelled the pleasing odor, Yahweh said in his heart. . .' This is not exactly the picture of the gods gathering like flies to the sacrifice that we find in Mesopotamian equivalents of the story, but it is reminiscent of it. Normally, however, biblical sacrificial language expresses somewhat more spiritual ideas.

The essence of any animal sacrifice is the bringing of the blood to the altar. Leviticus 17:10f. says, 'If any man of the house of Israel or of the sojourners among them eats any blood, I will set my face against that person who eats blood. . . For the life of the flesh is in the blood; and I have given it for you upon the altar to make atonement for your souls; for it is the blood that makes atonement, by reason of the life'. It also seems from this chapter that any animal that *can* be sacrificed *must* be killed in this way. In all sacrifices, certain entrails belong to God, and have to be burned on the altar. At least according to Leviticus, only a priest can approach the altar, so only a priest can sacrifice; his payment is some further part of the animal.

Leviticus 1 describes the 'burnt offering', and this is the most common sacrifice in regular Temple worship; the victim has to be a male animal, and is entirely burned on the altar. This sacrifice was also often used in cleansing rituals. The 'peace offering' is described in Leviticus 3; the person bringing the offering here receives most of it back for food. Leviticus 7 subdivides the peace offering into 'thank offering', 'free will offering', or 'votive offering'. The 'sin offering' is described in Leviticus 4–5; its main purpose is evidently to remove impurities, either in the sanctuary or 'if anyone sins unwittingly' or has forgotten some vow, or in certain cleansing rituals; the sin offering often accompanies a burnt offering. Leviticus 5–6 further mentions a 'guilt offering', to overcome desecration or perjury. Apart from these animal offerings there are cereal offerings. One notes that none of these sacrifices really deal with what we would call crimes. It seems that crimes committed against other people are simply to be dealt with by criminal law; and 'the person who does anything with a high hand . . . reviles Yahweh, and that person shall be cut off from among his people . . . His iniquity shall be upon him' (Numbers 15:30ff.).

The daily ritual in the Temple includes burnt offerings at morning and evening, and incense and cereal offerings, with more elaborate arrangements for Sabbaths, new moons, and festivals. One notes that the normal anthropomorphic accounts of temple rituals from the ancient world, involving, for example, washing and feeding a statue of a god, are here much curtailed. Leviticus 16 describes the ritual for the Day of Atonement: the high priest offers one sin offering for himself and another for the people, and brings the blood into the Holy of Holies, where the 'ark' is kept, to cleanse this most sacred area. He then places his hands on a living 'scapegoat', confesses the people's sins over it and sends it away into the wilderness: 'the goat shall bear all their iniquities upon him to a solitary land' (or, in other verses, 'to Azazel').

The various great events of Israelite history are frequently described as accompanied by sacrifices. For example, the departure for Egypt (Exodus 12) is marked by the sacrifice of a lamb, the charter for the ritual slaying of the Passover lamb, commemorating the daubing of the lintels of the Israelite houses with blood so that Yahweh would 'pass over' them when killing the Egyptian firstborn. Other sacrifices similarly mark the covenant at Sinai (Exodus 24), the consecration of Solomon's Temple (I Kings 8), and the Israelite restoration to Jerusalem after the exile (Ezra 3).

Christian readers have sometimes maintained that the Hebrew Bible's atoning, cleansing and expiating sacrifices indicate a mechanical attitude to religion. It has already been noted, however, that, according to the Pentateuchal laws, there is no mechanical way of atoning for sins committed 'with a high hand'. Other texts, too, express some doubts about sacrifices. Psalm 51 says: 'For you have no delight in sacrifice; / were I to give a burnt offering you would not be pleased. / The sacrifice acceptable to God is a broken spirit; / a broken and contrite heart, O God, you will not despise'. Amos 5:21ff. and some other prophetic texts come close to rejecting the whole apparatus of Israelite worship as a camouflage for a corrupt social order. Other, more spiritual modes of atonement are at least hinted at. In the fourth 'Servant Song' of Isaiah 53, the writer says, of himself, or perhaps of Israel: '. . . he poured out his soul to death, / and was numbered with the transgressors; / yet he bore the sin of many, / and made intercession for the transgressors'. The accounts of the martyrdoms of Eleazar and the mother with her seven sons, in the second and fourth Books of Maccabees, in the Apocrypha, show that such deaths, in 'witness' to God's law, were also coming to be thought of as atoning for the rest of Israel.

In the Gospels, Jesus seems to think of his own destiny along similar lines. Mark 10:45: 'For the Son of Man' (which here seems to mean simply 'I') 'also came not to be served but to serve, and to give his life as a ransom for many', may not be a direct allusion to Isaiah 53, but it is not dissimilar from it; it has been suggested that Jesus also had in mind the supposed violent fate of the earlier prophets, which he mentions elsewhere. The exact biblical background of Jesus' words at the Last Supper is not quite certain, but 'This cup is the new covenant in my blood' (I Corinthians 11:25) presumably means that Jesus expects his death will somehow inaugurate a new, or at least restored, relationship between God and Israel, as the Sinai covenant and its sacrifice had done. Mark's account of the Last Supper continues, 'Truly, I say to you, I shall not drink again of the fruit of the vine until that day when I drink it new in the kingdom of God' (14:25), which certainly seems to indicate some such idea.

Paul's writings have provided much of the basis for the Christian doctrine of the atonement. In many different passages he speaks of Jesus' death as an 'expiation' or a 'reconciliation' to God, or a 'redemption', or with various other metaphors drawn from the biblical sacrificial vocabulary. The background of some passages is clear, e.g. I Corinthians 5:7: 'Christ our paschal lamb has been sacrificed', but we are less clear about others. Romans 3:21ff. says: '[All men] are justified by [God's] grace as a gift, through the redemption which is in Christ Jesus, whom God put forward as an expiation by his blood, to be received by faith. . .' 'Expiation' here does not necessarily imply any substitutionary atonement, as often assumed. It may be an allusion to the 'mercy seat' in the Holy of Holies of the Temple, which was sprinkled with blood on the Day of Atonement; the Septuagint uses the same Greek word for that as Paul uses here for 'expiation'. Whatever the exact background of such passages, we should beware of pressing his sacrificial metaphors too hard, as sometimes seems to happen with 'doctrines of the atonement'. Such metaphors also appear in Hebrews, where the central type of Jesus is the high priest performing the Day of Atonement ritual: '[Christ] entered once for all into the Holy Place, taking not the blood of goats and calves but his own blood, thus securing an eternal redemption' (9:12).

Purity and holiness

These concepts, and their opposites, impurity and profanity, have been shown by anthropologists to characterize religions throughout the world. Emile Durkheim, in *The Elementary Forms of the Religious Life* (London, 1915), claimed that it was above all agreement as to what was sacred and what was profane that constituted a particular church or religion. Mary Douglas, in *Purity and Danger* (London, 1966), has discussed the classifications of pure and impure in the Pentateuch against the background of similar demarcations in many other societies. To people outside a particular society such classifications are likely to appear arbitrary; but within the society they come to seem natural, and within a society with a scholarly class, like the Jewish one, they can be the object of an elaborate science. To this day the Jewish religion puts great emphasis on ritual purity in choice and preparation of food, sexual behaviour, and many other areas of life. It is often suggested that the biblical rules on foods reflect common-sense health precautions in the climatic conditions of the Middle East, but it also seems that binary classifications like the biblical ones into pure and impure reflect a deep-seated human desire to understand and control the world by arranging it. Some biblical prohibitions may also have arisen from an attempt to demarcate what was Israelite from what was Canaanite. The rather curious 'You shall not boil a kid in its mother's milk' (Exodus 23:19), which has become the basis of a Jewish dietary rule about not mixing meat and milk, apparently refers to a type of Canaanite sacrifice.

The biblical purity rules include: Leviticus 11, on clean and unclean animals; 12, on childbirth; and 15, on sexual and other discharges from the body. Note also the ritual aspects of holy war: Deuteronomy 20 says much about the sacred aspect of the ancient Israelite army; and 23:9ff. about purity within the army camp – parallels to such ideas have been found in Roman and other ancient military customs. Haggai 2:10ff. gives an intriguing example of a priestly response on a purity question: does contact with sacrificed meat make other foods holy? (answer: no); does contact with a corpse make these foods unclean? (answer: yes). This anticipates the purity debates of the later Pharisees, which have left traces in the New Testament and are referred to at length in the Mishnah (of about 200 AD). We also now have many purity rules in the Dead Sea Scrolls, especially the 'Temple Scroll', which gives a sort of blueprint for a totally pure restored Jerusalem and Temple in the future.

Jesus' attitude to purity rules, at least as they were interpreted by the Pharisees, is presented in the Gospels as being partly critical. In Mark 7:1ff. the Pharisees see that 'some of his disciples ate with hands defiled, that is unwashed'. Jesus quotes Isaiah 29:13 against them and adds, 'You leave the commandment of God and hold fast the tradition of men'. Later he says, 'What comes out of a man is what defiles a man. For from within, out of the heart of a man, come evil thoughts, fornication, theft, murder, adultery. . .' In the early Christian movement the question very soon arose of how far gentile converts need keep the Jewish law, especially the purity rules; Paul campaigned vigorously against any such requirement (see especially Galatians). Hebrews 10 presents the view that, since Christ has 'offered for all time a single sacrifice for sins', Christians can draw near to God 'with our hearts sprinkled clean from an evil conscience and our bodies washed with pure water'.

Holiness is of course the special quality of God throughout the Bible, and Rudolf Otto, in *The Idea of the Holy* (1923), claimed that an experience of holiness as the 'numinous', or 'wholly other', was the essence of all religion. The Hebrew Bible relates a number of theophanies, or appearances of God: as a 'smoking fire pot and flaming torch' to Abraham in Genesis 15, and as 'three men' in 18; at the top of a ladder to Jacob in Genesis 28; in the burning bush to Moses in Exodus 3; in the 'still small voice' to Elijah in I Kings 19; in the vision of Yahweh in the Temple in Isaiah 6; in the rather more surreal vision of the 'chariot' in Ezekiel 1; and so on. Elaborate visions of the heavens and the heavenly court became a normal feature of Jewish apocalyptic (e.g. Daniel 7; and cf. much of Revelation). The New Testament also records many numinous experiences: Jesus' vision at his baptism of the heavens opening and the Spirit descending on him like a dove (Mark 1:10f.; the story seems to allude to the Spirit of God 'hovering' over the waters in Genesis 1:2); the transfiguration of Jesus on a 'high mountain' before Peter, James and John (Mark 9:2ff., a story clearly intended to recall Moses' and Elijah's experiences); the stories of Jesus' appearances after his resurrection; various visions in Acts; Paul's 'visions and revelations of the Lord' (II Corinthians 12:1); and his references to 'spiritual gifts' in the early Christian communities.

The above are, so to speak, accounts of extraordinary experiences of holiness. Israelite society also, like all others, accepted certain regular places, times, rituals, objects and customs as being holy. Many of the shrines in Israel seem to have been taken over directly from earlier cultures in Palestine; the story of Jacob's ladder in Genesis 28, for example, mentioned above, can be understood as a patriarchal vetting of an older Canaanite shrine at Bethel for Israelite use. Even the Jerusalem Temple may well have replaced an earlier Jebusite sanctuary; the story that God, through Nathan the prophet, forbade David to build the Temple (II Samuel 7) may indicate some doubt whether the Israelites should have done this. However, some sort of building was also necessary to house (and perhaps domesticate) the 'ark', a mysterious sacred object from an earlier, tribal phase of Israelite society, which is said to have caused havoc to the Philistines when they captured it (I Samuel 4ff.). During the monarchy spasmodic efforts were made by the 'good' kings to close down local sanctuaries in favour of the Jerusalem Temple, and the Deuteronomist develops a view of God's 'name' dwelling in the Temple to justify such policies. The legal passages of the Pentateuch not only require this centralization of worship, but lay down rules for daily and festival ritual quite minutely; this uniform legislation hardly reflects the diverse manifestations of the sacred in early and monarchic Israel, though it may well have become the norm for Jerusalem after the exile. Leviticus 17–26, often called today the 'Holiness Code' because of its demands to 'be holy, for I, Yahweh, your God am holy', may particularly express the religious spirit of this later period.

The New Testament assumes many of the Hebrew Bible's views on holiness, but also reflects beliefs in Jesus as a particularly or even uniquely holy person. Jesus makes no such direct claims for himself, but is frequently called holy by others, including the demons he exorcizes. He may not explicitly query normal Jewish ideas about holiness, but he does question external holiness, or piety, in people. His association with profane types such as tax collectors and prostitutes, and his claim that such people will 'enter the kingdom of heaven' before the pious, apparently without needing to repent first, constitute at least an implied criticism. His attitude to the Temple also seems partly critical. The 'cleansing' of the Temple (Mark 11:15ff., etc.) does not necessarily indicate more than a dislike of commercialized religion. However, the mysterious saying, 'Destroy this temple that is made with hands, and in three days I will build another, not made with hands' (Mark 14:58, which may be an allusion to the model of the tent revealed to Moses at Sinai), *may* indicate not just doubt about the worth of the present Temple, but an expectation that, in the Messianic days that Jesus himself might introduce, a heavenly Temple would replace it.

At all events, circumstances, particularly the greater success of Christianity among gentiles than among Jews, soon weakened Christian sense of the holiness of the Temple; and of course its destruction in 70 AD made it of only 'Messianic' relevance for Jews also. By this stage Christians were convinced that the 'Holy Spirit' had now been 'poured out' on them (as prophesied in Joel 2:28), and that through the Spirit they had direct access to God: 'When we cry, "Abba! Father!" it is the Spirit himself bearing witness with our spirit that we are children of God . . .' (Romans 8:15f.; see also p. 77). In much of the New Testament Christians are called 'the saints', and Paul in particular has a remarkably concrete sense of the Christian community as the new locus of God's holiness.

The Kingdom of God and the Messiah

As we have seen, the image of God as king is quite common in the Bible, as it is throughout the ancient Near East. It is not quite clear what this image implies for the Israelites' view of their own kings. All Near Eastern kings were considered divine in some sense, and the Israelite kings would tend to be thought the same. Some biblical texts, especially the enthronement Psalms, and Messianic passages in the prophets, may imply such a notion. On the other hand, the Deuteronomistic historian, and many of the prophets, could be highly critical of both the institution of monarchy and individual kings, and the somewhat heightened royal language of some Psalms and prophecies must be balanced against other more penitential texts. Nevertheless, there *is* a certain continuity of imagery from, for example, Egyptian and Mesopotamian enthronement texts and oracles to the Israelite royal and Messianic ideology.

In I Samuel 8, the 'elders of Israel' ask Samuel to give them a king. When Samuel consults God on the matter he replies: 'Hearken to the voice of the people in all that they say to you; for they have not rejected you, but they have rejected me from being king over them'. Even though, in some of the following chapters, God seems to accept the proposal more enthusiastically, the Bible from the start sees some tensions between the Israelite monarchy and God's 'kingship'. This tension reappears in II Samuel 7, where David, having built his palace in Jerusalem, proposes to build a temple for the 'ark of God', but God replies through the prophet Nathan: 'Would you build me a house to dwell in? I have not dwelt in a house since the day I brought up the people of Israel from Egypt to this day, but I have been moving about in a tent for my dwelling'. Nevertheless, God then guarantees a successor to David: 'He shall build a house for my name, and I will establish the throne of his kingdom for ever'. In time Solomon succeeds to David (not without some fairly ruthless political manoeuvring), and proceeds to build the 'house of Yahweh', quite obviously following Canaanite models and using Canaanite expertise. After a dedication in I Kings 8, very reminiscent of the style of Deuteronomy, God says to Solomon, 'I have consecrated this house which you have built, and put my name there for ever' (I Kings 9:3). This dual guarantee, of the continuing dynasty of David and of the impregnability of Jerusalem, or 'Zion', appears very frequently in the Psalms and some of the prophets. The city itself can be pictured in almost mythical terms: 'There is a river whose streams make glad the city of God, / the holy habitation of the Most High. / God is in the midst of her, she shall not be moved . . . ' (Psalm 46:4).

The Hebrew term 'Messiah' means 'anointed', and most often in the Hebrew Bible refers to an Israelite king, present or anticipated. Because the Christian tradition has used this title (especially in its Greek form 'Christ') so exclusively of Jesus, one can easily miss the fact that the Hebrew 'Messianic' texts almost always refer to an actual king known at the time of writing, or at least to someone expected to become king fairly shortly. Even such a famous 'Messianic prophecy' as Isaiah 7:10ff.: 'Behold a young woman shall conceive and bear a son, and shall call his name Immanuel . . .' quite clearly in its context refers to events during the reign of King Ahaz of Judah (possibly the 'young woman' was the king's pregnant wife); and, further, it is not strictly Messianic in any sense, because Isaiah does not say the son will become king. 'Second Isaiah' can call the foreign king Cyrus of Persia God's anointed, because he sees Cyrus as acting in favour of Israel. Other well-known 'Messianic' texts occur in Zechariah, but, at least in Zechariah 1–8, the prophet is clearly speaking of circumstances soon after the restoration of the Israelites to Jerusalem, when one Joshua had been anointed as high priest, and it was hoped (unrealistically, as it turned out) that Zerubbabel would be a new Israelite king.

Daniel 9:25ff. speaks of 'the coming of an anointed one, a prince', but here, too, the numerical calculations in this passage suggest the author had some definite figure in mind. The 'one like a son of man' of Daniel 7:13 seems more a sort of angelic heavenly representative of Israel than a king, and is not said to be anointed. In the 'intertestamental' Jewish texts, such as the Psalms of Solomon and the Dead Sea Scrolls, 'indefinite' future Messianic figures *do* sometimes appear. It should be pointed out, too, that many of the biblical texts that originally referred to 'definite' Messiahs were reinterpreted in this period as referring to an 'indefinite' future Messiah, as we can see from the Dead Sea Scrolls, and from the Targums (discussed on pp. 109–11).

In the Synoptic Gospels Jesus frequently speaks of the 'kingdom of God' (or of 'heaven') as being 'at hand', or 'among you', and most of his parables seem intended to illustrate the paradoxical nature of this concept. Quite possibly 'reign of God' would be a better translation, i.e. a condition of the world in which God's will has direct effect. The concept may be, as often claimed, an apocalyptic one, but this does not necessarily mean that Jesus expected the kingdom to come about through some violent intervention by God in the world. Apocalyptic is more a sort of visionary equivalent of expected historical events than it is a literal prediction of what will happen (see the discussion on Jesus' supposed apocalyptic outlook on pp. 50–5 above). A similar caution needs to be used in discussing whether Jesus 'claimed to be the Messiah', or spoke of himself as the 'Son of Man' in something like the sense of Daniel 7:13. The relevant texts in the Gospels are hard to reconcile, no doubt because they reflect rather different understandings of what these terms meant. We can at least say that in the Gospels Jesus uses somewhat visionary imagery to convey a sense that God can and

will intervene in human events, and that in some way his own
life reflects such an intervention. It was the early Christians
who concluded, from studying the Hebrew Bible, that he *was*
the Messiah, the Son of David, the Son of Man, the Son of
God, etc., thereby hardening these images into 'titles'.

Suffering, exile, and restoration

The problem of suffering is, of course, one of the most profound of human enigmas, at both personal and conceptual
levels. The Bible tries to 'explain' it in a number of rather different ways, all of which have some sort of parallel in other
cultures and religions. According to the first creation account
of Genesis, in 1:1–2:4, God 'sees' that each stage of creation
is 'good'; and he gives humans authority to 'fill the earth and
subdue it'. According to the following creation account, man
was first put into the 'garden of Eden, to till it and keep it',
but told: 'of the tree of the knowledge of good and evil you
shall not eat, for on the day that you eat of it you shall die'
(2:15ff.). The account in Genesis 3 of the woman's being persuaded to disobey this command by the serpent, of her persuading her husband, and of God's punishing all three with
suffering, can be interpreted at several levels. If we assume that
humans' desire for knowledge, including sexual knowledge, is
an inevitable part of growing up, then the story tells us that
such knowledge involves a painful separation from children's
state of natural bliss. If we note that many other cultures have
myths of the jealousy of the gods, we may conclude that
Yahweh is here making humans realize their limitations, or even
just acting as a tyrant. If we are familiar with myths of the
trickery of the gods, we might conclude that humans do indeed get what the serpent promises them, namely to know good
and evil, but in so doing miss out on the even greater good
of living forever. At all events, Genesis 3 has become one of
the most famous, or notorious, 'explanations' of the origin of
sin and suffering (some interpretations of the story in English
literature will be discussed on pp. 134–8). It is followed by
the equally well known stories of Cain killing Abel, of God's

destruction by flood of all men except those preserved in Noah's ark and of the Tower of Babel, all with equally complex levels of meaning, which between them 'explain' the violence, fragility, and chaos of human life (and in all of which God seems to play a rather ambiguous moral role).

The historical books of the Hebrew Bible usually discern a simple cause and effect relation between sin and suffering. In Numbers 14f., spies are sent into the land of Palestine for forty days, but of them only Caleb and Joshua urge the Israelites to occupy the land immediately. The people believe the other spies' 'evil report' of the land and its giants, whereupon God curses them to wander for forty years in the wilderness, until all that faithless generation (other than Caleb and Joshua) are dead. The 'Deuteronomistic history' interprets all of Israelite history from Joshua down to the fall of the monarchy as an alternation of prosperity and suffering, according to the righteousness or sinfulness of the people, and especially of their 'judges' and kings. Its interpretation extends on a larger historical scale the normal prophetic claim that God would punish or reward the people as a whole for their leaders' actions.

The Deuteronomist views the collapse of the monarchy as the fitting final punishment for Israel's long history of faithlessness. This possibility had long been foreseen by prophets, but Isaiah at least had suggested that even so 'a remnant will return, the remnant of Jacob, to the mighty God' (10:21). Jeremiah ventured a long-term prophecy at the moment of collapse: 'This whole land shall become a ruin and a waste, and these nations shall serve the king of Babylon seventy years. Then after seventy years are completed, I will punish the king of Babylon and that nation, the land of the Chaldeans, for their iniquity, says Yahweh, making the land an everlasting waste' (25:11f.; see also 29:10). As it happened, after about fifty years Cyrus, the king of Persia, did conquer Babylon, and allowed the various nations exiled in Babylonia to return to their territories. 'Second Isaiah' takes this to mean 'that [Israel] has received from Yahweh's hand double for all her sins' (40:2). He also believes that Cyrus, 'his anointed' (= Messiah) was doing this 'for the sake of my servant Jacob, and

Israel my chosen' (45:1ff.), although Cyrus' own account, in an inscription known as the 'Cyrus Cylinder', suggests wider religious considerations (including special concern to restore the worship of Marduk in Babylon).

During the exile, another prophet, Ezekiel, began to question such views of communal solidarity in suffering. 'The word of Yahweh came to me again: "What do you mean by repeating this proverb concerning the land of Israel, 'The fathers have eaten sour grapes, and the children's teeth are set on edge'? Behold, all souls are mine; the soul of the father as well as the soul of the son is mine: the soul that sins shall die" ' (18:1ff.). Similar individualistic views appear frequently in the 'wisdom' literature: 'Be assured, an evil man will not go unpunished, / but those who are righteous will be delivered' (Proverbs, 11:21). Job's 'comforters' assure him that this is the case, and that therefore his sufferings must be punishment for some secret sin; but they also show some doubt whether men can know God's purposes, and even say: 'Behold, happy is the man whom God reproves; / therefore despise not the chastening of the Almighty' (5:17). Job, however, cannot accept that there can be any justification for suffering like his; the only 'solution' to his problem comes with his direct encounter with God: 'therefore I have uttered what I did not understand, / things too wonderful for me, which I did not know' (42:3).

The Hebrew Bible refers only very rarely to Satan as the cause of evil in the world. In the New Testament, however, Satan, or various other devils, are regularly said to be the cause of physical and mental illness, and therefore healings often consist in the casting out of devils. Jesus' exorcisms lead to controversy with Jewish leaders over whether he must be in league with the devils to be able to cast them out; in one response he claims: 'But if it is by the finger of God that I cast out demons, then the kingdom of God has come upon you' (Luke 11:20). This highly personified view of evil was evidently widespread in Jesus' day. Paul interprets various personal and circumstantial obstacles to his mission as being diabolical, and also sees the world as a whole as being somehow 'enslaved' to 'principalities and powers'; however Colossians 2:15 also claims that God, through Jesus' death on the cross, 'disarmed the principalities and powers and made a public example of them, triumphing over them in him'. In Romans Paul claims that 'sin came into the world through one man and death through sin, and so death spread to all men because all men sinned' (5:12). He is here referring to the 'original sin' of Adam, which was punished by mortality, but also believes that men in general deserve this punishment because they have all in fact sinned. An ambiguity in the Latin translations of this verse has led many Western Christians to believe that all men sinned 'in' Adam (see the further discussion of this passage on p. 112).

Wisdom

The Hebrew and Greek words translated by 'wisdom' cover a wide semantic field: 'skill', 'cleverness', 'coping with life', 'prudence', and so on. There is, however, in the Bible a 'wisdom tradition', which in many ways is universal, and comparable to very old traditions in other parts of the ancient Near East and elsewhere, but at the same time is the basis of many specifically biblical ideas. The traditional founder of 'wisdom' in Israel was Solomon: according to I Kings 3, God appeared to him in a dream at Gibeon and said, 'Ask what I shall give you', to which Solomon replied, 'I am but a little child. . . Give your servant therefore an understanding mind to govern your people, that I may discern between good and evil'. His wisdom is immediately demonstrated in his celebrated judgement between two prostitutes claiming the same child, and later we hear much of his scholarly reputation and research output. In later Jewish legend he is shown as putting his wisdom to some rather questionable magical uses. The wisdom tradition in the Bible is seen in Proverbs, Job and Ecclesiastes, but also in some Psalms, and in a more general way in many narrative and poetic texts. As most scholars define it, this tradition is not much concerned with God's promises to Israel or their fulfilment, or with the details of religious practice, or with questions of social justice. It aims rather to pass on timeless lessons of experience, so that readers can succeed in life, or at least cope with it. It can easily seem complacent, but can also produce Job's deeply unsettling questioning of God's justice, and Ecclesiastes' almost equally disturbing expressions of boredom with life. Finally, it can speculate about God's somewhat enigmatic presence in the beauty and order of the natural world, as in Proverbs 8:22ff., Job 28 and elsewhere, and such Psalms as 19: 'The heavens are telling the glory of God; / and the firmament proclaims his handiwork'.

The Jewish wisdom tradition continued on into the Hellenistic period (see Wisdom and Ecclesiasticus, among the Apocrypha), and seems to have been at least slightly influenced by Greek philosophical and religious ideas (or heavily influenced, if writers such as Philo of Alexandria can be considered part of the tradition). In the New Testament a perhaps surprising number of Jesus' sayings belong to the tradition: 'Do not lay up for yourselves treasures on earth, where moth and rust consume and where thieves break in and steal, but lay up for yourselves treasures in heaven' (Matthew 6:19f.). According to Luke 11:31, 'the queen of the South will arise at the judgement with the men of this generation and condemn them; for she came from the ends of the earth to hear the wisdom of Solomon, and behold, something greater than Solomon is here' (though perhaps this means that Jesus sees his own more 'prophetic' teaching about judgement as more important than 'wisdom'). In the Synoptics Jesus makes a striking, paradoxical, and even exclusive claim to wisdom at Matthew 11:25–7: 'I thank you Father, Lord of heaven and earth, that you have hidden these things from the wise and understanding and revealed them to babes. . . All things have been delivered to me by my Father; and no one knows the Son except the Father, and no one knows the Father except the Son and any one to whom the Son chooses to reveal him'.

Curiously enough 'wisdom' does not appear as such in John's Gospel. However, there is little doubt that John's identification of Jesus with 'the Word' in his prologue (1:1–18) is based partly on the tradition of personified Wisdom; it may possibly also owe something to Hellenistic Jewish developments of this tradition such as we find in Philo, and to speculations about the *memra*, or 'word' as a periphrasis for God, to be seen in the Targums. Wisdom *is* an important concept for Paul, and again it is sometimes a very personified concept. In I Corinthians 1:17ff. he gives a highly paradoxical account of the wisdom tradition:

Has not God made foolish the wisdom of the world? For since, in the wisdom of God, the world did not know God through wisdom, it pleased God through the folly of what we preach to save those who believe . . . we preach Christ crucified, a stumbling block to Jews and folly to Gentiles, but to those who are called, both Jews and Greeks, Christ the power of God and the wisdom of God.

Nevertheless, Paul, when 'forced' to 'speak as a fool' by the challenge of his opponents, gives an extraordinary account of his own initiation into wisdom: 'And I know that this man was caught up into Paradise − whether in the body or out of the body I do not know, God knows − and he heard things that cannot be told, which man may not utter' (II Corinthians 12:3f.). According to Ephesians the purpose of Paul's preaching was 'to make all men see what is the plan of the mystery hidden for ages in God who created all things; that through the church the manifold wisdom of God might now be made known to the principalities and powers in the heavenly places' (3:9f.). This text might also serve as a summary of the almost infinitely complex strands of interpretation and reinterpretation in biblical themes, which this chapter is intended to illustrate.

A comparison of spirits

Erich Auerbach began his famous survey of European literature from Homer to Virginia Woolf (*Mimesis: The Representation of Reality in Western Literature*, Princeton, New Jersey, 1953) with a comparison of an episode from the *Odyssey*, Book 19 (on the recognition of Odysseus by his old nurse Euryclea, from a scar on his thigh), with one from the Book of Genesis, Chapter 22 (the story of the sacrifice of Isaac). This comparison brought out very forcefully some differences between Homeric and biblical narrative styles. In this appendix to a chapter on

'Leading themes of the Bible', a comparison will be made between two passages of the Bible, one from Ezekiel and the other
from Paul's Epistle to the Romans. Both have to do with the
Spirit of God, one of the key biblical metaphors for the
presence of God in the world, in individuals and in communities. Together they illustrate both the continuities of
biblical thinking (which all the earlier sections of this chapter
have also emphasized), and certain notable transformations
which the Hebrew Bible's traditions undergo in the New
Testament.

Therefore say to the house of Israel, Thus says the God Yahweh: It
is not for your sake, O house of Israel, that I am about to act, but
for the sake of my holy name, which you have profaned among the
nations to which you came. And I will vindicate the holiness of my
great name, which has been profaned among the nations, and which
you have profaned among them; and the nations will know that I am
Yahweh, says the God Yahweh, when through you I vindicate my
holiness before their eyes. For I will take you from the nations, and
gather you from all the countries, and bring you into your own land.
I will sprinkle clean water upon you, and you shall be clean from your
uncleannesses, and from all your idols will I cleanse you. A new heart
I will give you, and a new spirit I will put within you; and I will take
out of your flesh the heart of stone and give you a heart of flesh.
And I will put my spirit within you, and cause you to walk in my
statutes and be careful to observe my ordinances. You shall dwell in
the land which I gave to your fathers; and you shall be my people,
and I will be your God. And I will deliver you from all your uncleannesses; and I will summon the grain and make it abundant and lay
no famine upon you. I will make the fruit of the tree and the increase
of the field abundant, and you will never again suffer the disgrace
of famine among the nations. Then you will remember your evil ways,
and your deeds that were not good; and you will loathe yourself for
your iniquities and your abominable deeds. It is not for your sake
that I will act, says Yahweh the God; let that be known to you. Be
ashamed and confounded for your ways, O house of Israel.
(Ezekiel 36:22–32)

We recall that Ezekiel delivered his prophecies among the
Israelite exiles in Babylonia. In the above prophecy, he
announces that God will in time lead his people back to their
land, and give prosperity to that land. However, this will not
be because of any merit on the part of the Israelites − they

have shown by their 'uncleannesses' that they have been rightly punished with exile. If God is to lead them back, then he will have first not only to wash them from their past profanities, but to give them 'a new heart' and 'a new spirit', virtually a new human nature. Only then will they be able to 'walk in his statutes', and 'loathe' themselves for their past iniquities. Further, God will be doing all this not for their sake, 'but for the sake of my holy name, which you have profaned among the nations to which you have come'.

It should be noted how the term for 'spirit' (*ruach*) is used in the Hebrew Bible. As Owen Barfield has perceptively pointed out, the Hebrew use of this word belongs to a world of primal participation in which natural phenomena like wind could also be experienced as essentially magical or divine in a way that cannot be properly recaptured by twentieth-century English readers ('The meaning of "literal" ', *Metaphor and Symbol*, ed. Basil Cottle and L. C. Knights, Bristol, 1960). Thus it can mean simply 'wind', but when it is used of God it means his 'breath' or 'power', and it is used of God in three contexts especially: of God's creation (as in Genesis 1:2); of his inspiring or empowering leaders, prophets and other charismatic figures; and of his presence with his people in some future restored state, as in this passage of Ezekiel, but also in, for example, Joel 2:28f., where that presence will be manifested in 'prophetic' ways:

And it will come to pass afterward, / that I will pour out my spirit on all flesh; / your sons and your daughters shall prophesy, / your old men shall dream dreams, / and your young men shall see visions. / Even upon the manservants and maidservants / in those days, I will pour out my spirit.

This last passage may lead us to note by comparison some of the limitations in Ezekiel's vision of the future. Although such a dramatic intervention by God will be necessary before he can lead the Israelites back to their land, their life there will have a curiously static quality: in spite of having the very spirit of God, which could lead them to the transformed society which Joel evidently thinks possible, for Ezekiel their task will simply be to carry out God's law as they should have done in the first place, and to loathe their earlier failures.

There is therefore now no condemnation for those who are in Christ Jesus. For the law of the Spirit of life in Christ Jesus has set me free from the law of sin and death. For God has done what the law, weakened by the flesh, could not do: sending his own Son in the likeness of sinful flesh and for sin [or 'and as a sin offering'], he condemned sin in the flesh, in order that the just requirement of the law might be fulfilled in us, who walk not according to the flesh but according to the Spirit. For those who live according to the flesh set their minds on the things of the flesh, but those who live according to the Spirit set their minds on the things of the Spirit. To set the mind on the flesh is death, but to set the mind on the Spirit is life and peace. For the mind that is set on the flesh is hostile to God; it does not submit to God's law, indeed it cannot; and those who are in the flesh cannot please God.

But you are not in the flesh, you are in the Spirit, if in fact the Spirit of God dwells in you. Anyone who does not have the Spirit of Christ does not belong to him. But if Christ is in you, although your bodies are dead because of sin, your spirits are alive because of righteousness. If the Spirit of him who raised Jesus from the dead dwells in you, he who raised Christ Jesus from the dead will give life to your mortal bodies also through his Spirit which dwells in you.

So then, brethren, we are debtors not to the flesh, to live according to the flesh — for if you live according to the flesh you will die, but if by the Spirit you put to death the deeds of the body you will live. For all who are led by the Spirit of God are sons of God. For you did not receive the spirit of slavery to fall back into fear, but you have received the spirit of sonship. When we cry, 'Abba! Father!' it is the Spirit himself bearing witness with our spirit that we are children of God, and if children, then heirs, heirs of God and fellow heirs with Christ, provided we suffer with him in order that we may also be glorified with him.

I consider that the sufferings of this present time are not worth comparing with the glory that is to be revealed to us. For the creation waits with eager longing for the revealing of the sons of God; for the creation was subjected to futility, not of its own will but by the will of him who subjected it in hope; because the creation itself will be set free from its bondage to decay and obtain the glorious freedom of the sons of God. We know that the whole creation has been groaning in travail together until now; and not only the creation, but we ourselves, who have the first fruits of the Spirit, groan inwardly as we await for adoption as sons, the redemption of our bodies.

(Romans 8: 1–23)

Paul was writing this, as an active member of the 'open'

urban society of the Roman Empire, in the full excitement of the first Christian generation. In spite of an almost obsessive harping on 'sin', 'death', 'flesh', 'suffering' and 'groaning', he is certain that the Spirit of God is not merely a promise for the future, but a power already able to transform lives. However, the very contrast between 'flesh' and 'spirit' in this passage already shows us that we have here to do with a cultural and personal outlook quite different from Ezekiel's. For Ezekiel, the 'heart of flesh' and the 'new spirit' which God will give are virtually synonymous expressions. For Paul, 'if you live according to the flesh you will die, but if by the Spirit you put to death the deeds of the body you will live'. Ezekiel looked forward to an Israel at last able to 'walk in my statutes', but for Paul 'God has done what the law, weakened by the flesh, could not do': he has sent his Son 'in the likeness of sinful flesh' to 'condemn sin in the flesh' (the exact meaning of this passage is somewhat obscure; hence the alternative translations offered by the Revised Standard Version). One might say that both Ezekiel and Paul, perhaps rather wistfully, have concluded that the 'law' is an impossible ideal for normal humanity; but the means by which they think God can help men out are very different.

God's motives and ultimate intentions are also very different in the two cases. For Ezekiel, God will act in order to stop his name being profaned any more among the nations, by his unworthy people. For Paul, God has acted so as to allow all men to be his sons, rather than his slaves; and further so that 'the whole creation', hitherto 'groaning in travail together', may be 'set free from its bondage to decay and obtain the glorious liberty of the children of God'. He even mentions the possibility of 'the redemption of our bodies'. This is a somewhat more exalted vision of the possibilities for humanity.

Finally, one must make the perhaps obvious point that, for Paul, God has sent a quite specific person to carry out his intentions, namely Jesus. This person, Paul believes, is not merely God's 'Christ', or Messiah, but in some sense 'his own Son'. Paul alternates between the expressions 'Spirit of God' and 'Spirit of Christ' to describe the power by which God brings men's spirits 'alive'. Thus Christ's special relationship to God, he believes, has been demonstrated by the fact that it was God's Spirit who raised him from the dead. Ezekiel would have had little difficulty understanding any of Paul's imagery here (indeed, Paul may well be drawing on Ezekiel for much of it), but he might have found Paul's identification of the sending of God's Spirit with the coming of Jesus premature. Both visionaries, perhaps, have their own kinds of limitation. And, in case we are tempted to see Paul's vision as inevitably more exalted than any vision in the Hebrew Bible, it is worth remembering that Joel anticipates a good deal of what Paul believed had in fact happened.

Chapter 4

Interpretation of the Bible

The reader who has come so far will be conscious of the fact that even the word 'interpretation' is ambiguous in the context of the Bible. Does it refer to the historical study of the social and cultic environment from which the writings are assumed to have come, to the modes of literary and stylistic analysis by which different presumed authors or schools of thought may be distinguished and to the 'intentions' of the writers so deduced? Or does it set aside such speculative and essentially controversial groping after what may lie behind the texts and accept instead those texts themselves as its basic material? Clearly, both approaches have their value. It is impossible to ignore the fact that the documents of the Hebrew Bible were written and rewritten over a span of perhaps 1000 years, and that even the earliest surviving books may have other even earlier texts behind them – indeed, there are references in the existing texts to such missing, or possibly mythical, books as the Book of the Battles of Yahweh and the Book of Yashar. Nevertheless, clearly in a work such as the present one, it is the second approach which must now take precedence, with its concentration on the traditional form of the writings making up the book that has so decisively influenced the growth of European civilization.

As we have seen illustrated again and again, central to any such interpretation is a recognition of the degree to which the Bible is 'metafictional'. That is, it is a book about other books. The texts make constant and repeated reference to events or sayings in preceding books, either to confirm their significance, or to reinterpret them as part of a new pattern – always with the underlying implication that such references explore the wider pattern of God's mysterious dealings with his people, whether they should be defined as Jews, Christians, or the whole of humanity. It should therefore be obvious that any idea of a clear distinction in the Bible between the original literal meaning and a later process of commentary and interpretation is historically quite misleading. Right from the beginning, the narratives, prophecies, hymns, prescriptions and wisdom literature that make up the biblical writings were inseparably intertwined with interpretation and comment: not only through the overt process of continuous commentary and reference that we know as midrash, but also through the actual ordering and structure of the narratives themselves.

Midrash

'What is Torah?' asks one rabbi in a passage from the Babylonian Talmud (Kiddushin 49b), and Torah, remember, stands here, as it often does, as a collective designation for the whole of the Jewish Scriptures, and not merely the Pentateuch. And the answer comes: 'It is interpretation of the Torah' — *midrash Torah* in the Hebrew. This midrash technique and process, this mode of Jewish interpretation, plays such a vital part in the making of Scripture, that we can understand it against the background of the power at work in the putting together of a biblical text, in the transmission of that text, and in subsequent post-canonical interpretations of that text. It is the germ, the seed of Scripture, and understanding it will help us in our reading of the Old and New Testaments, since with its aid we can see the text with the eyes of the midrashist, who was at one and the same time maker and interpreter, and used his skill to build up his text from traditional material, and — after it had been constructed — to read something new out of the text for each succeeding generation.
(Michael Wadsworth, 'Making and interpreting scripture', in *Ways of Reading the Bible*. ed. Wadsworth, Brighton, 1981, p. 8).

The text of the Bible as it has been transmitted to us is at once self-conscious and reflexive to an extraordinary degree. 'How is it written of the Son of Man, that he should suffer many things and be treated with contempt?' asks Jesus (Mark 9:12–13). 'I tell you that Elijah has come and they did to him whatever they pleased, as it is written of him.' Since Elijah, we are told, was taken up into heaven by a whirlwind (II Kings 2:11), he was held to belong, with Enoch and Melchizedek, to those who had not tasted death. It was, therefore, appropriate that Malachi in the closing words of the Old Testament should have prophesied his reappearance as a herald of the Messiah (Malachi 4:4–5). There is, however, no reference in either the Old Testament or, so far as can be discovered, in the Jewish tradition as a whole, to Elijah's suffering and being rejected as an essential feature of his ministry – as distinct from his persecution by Ahab and Jezebel. What Jesus – or the Gospel writer – seems to have done at this point is to link Elijah, as the 'type' of the prophet, or servant of God, with the 'suffering servant' passages in Isaiah 53, in order to give a meaningful shape to the life and death of John the Baptist (Stephen Prickett, *Words and the Word*, Cambridge, 1986, p. 23). That casual phrase, 'as it is written of him', is the signal for linking the narrative of II Kings with the prophecies of Isaiah and Malachi, so as to explain the disturbing and seemingly random flux of contemporary events. The example is one of thousands, but it illustrates well how deeply the New Testament interpretation of the Old is rooted in traditional Hebrew methods of exegesis, whereby the past and present are linked together in a meaningful chain of event and commentary.

Internal interpretations

One of the most significant critical developments of the past few years has been a growing appreciation of the fact that, so far from being crude compilations of early myths and folk-stories, the documents of the Hebrew Bible are in fact highly sophisticated literary texts providing their own commentary through internal rhetorical techniques. For instance, allegory, and its various derivatives, such as typology, which were to play such a major part in biblical interpretation from New Testament times onwards, were already well known to the authors of the Old Testament. Indeed, there is evidence of the use of allegory in pre-biblical Babylonian and Egyptian texts. If the prophet Nathan's allegory of the rich man and the poor man's lamb (II Samuel 12:1–14) at first catches David by surprise, neither he nor the reader has any difficulty in understanding the technique for applying its moral to his actions towards Uriah and Bathsheba. Similarly, Jesus' parables depend for their effect on his audience's familiarity with allegory, a familiarity presumably derived from such Old Testament examples.

Because it was to form a staple part of later processes of interpretation, the importance of such literary devices as allegory in the Bible has long been recognized. What until recently has been less recognized is that the very features taken by form critics to be evidence of textual emendation and collation may on the contrary be the product of conscious rhetorical techniques. As Robert Alter, one of the leading literary scholars of the Bible, puts it, 'One only has to scan the history of a recent literary genre, the novel, to see how rapidly formal conventions shift, and to realize that elements like disjunction, interpolation, repetition, contrastive styles, which in biblical scholarship were long deemed signs of a defective text, may be perfectly deliberate components of the literary artwork, and recognized as such by the audience for which it is intended' ('Introduction to the Old Testament', in *The Literary Guide to the Bible*, Cambridge, Massachusetts, 1987, p. 27).

Gabriel Josipovici, for instance, has convincingly shown, in *The Book of God,* how this is likely to be the case in Genesis with the story of Joseph. As we saw in chapter 2, a common view of critical scholars is that the Joseph stories are 'didactic narrative, such as we find in Wisdom literature', calling for 'a totally different judgement from that passed on the stories about Abraham, Isaac, or Jacob, which are to some extent composed of cultic or local units of tradition'. In contrast, Josipovici points out that Joseph's story is only an episode in the larger story of Jacob, and that if this is understood, the story of Judah and Tamar (Genesis 38), which had long been regarded as just such an interpolated 'local unit of tradition', makes a quite different kind of sense. Judah, after all, is no incidental figure in the Joseph story. It is he who, though conniving at Joseph being cast into the pit, saves his life by having him sold to the Midianite slavers. It is he also who later pleads for his brother Benjamin's life before the still unrecognized Joseph.

His role as the defender of his two younger brothers is the more significant, of course, when we realize that the story of Tamar concerns the unlikely course of his own descendants. With the death of his sons Er and then Onan he is left childless except for Shelah (of whom it is merely recorded that Tamar is 'not given to him to wife'). It is only because he is tricked into getting Tamar with child, it seems, that his line is perpetuated at all. The full irony of this lies altogether outside Genesis, when we realize that the apparently triumphant and justified Joseph is the only one of his brothers *not* to found a tribe; and though his sons, Ephraim and Manasseh, are elevated by Jacob's blessing (Genesis 48) to the same patriarchal status as their uncles, it will be from the tribe of Judah that David and the Hebrew golden age will eventually come. Moreover it is only the tribes of Judah and Benjamin that will survive the Babylonian captivity as a remnant of the faithful. Even Josipovici omits to mention the further irony that, in both the lineages of Jesus given in the New Testament (Matthew 1 and Luke 3), the descent of Jesus (through Joseph!) is given as via David to Pharez, the child by incest of Judah and Tamar. Matthew, moreover, even draws attention to a further irregularity in the line of Jesus' descent (1:6): Solomon is the son of David by Bathsheba, the death of whose husband, Uriah the Hittite, he had engineered, thereby earning Nathan's denunciation. The exact degree to which the various writers have contributed to the wider mysterious pattern of what Josipovici has called the 'rhythm' of the Bible is a matter of debate, but to see such ironies as nothing more than the accidental product of textual interpolation and juxtaposition is to shut our eyes to some of the Bible's most subtle yet powerful internal commentaries.

The New Testament as an interpretation of the Old

Nowhere are these implicit commentaries more apparent than in the ordering of the biblical books themselves. As we have seen, the arrangement of the Old Testament differentiates itself sharply from the Hebrew Bible, in spite of the near identity of their contents, and points by implication towards what is

to follow. In the New Testament this hitherto implicit interpretative pattern becomes explicit. Taking its cue from the
genealogies at the beginning of Matthew and Luke, it continues
directly with Jesus' own frequent commentaries on and interpretations of the Hebrew scriptures — punctuated with the constant refrain, 'this he said/did in order that the scriptures might
be fulfilled'. A new element is also present, that of mystery,
of a hidden secret known only to the initiates — those with
'ears to hear' and 'eyes to see'. As was essential if the
recalcitrant material of the Old Testament was to be made to
fit the pattern now imposed upon it by the New, the early Christians, so far from being the literalists they are sometimes
assumed to be, were quick to play down literal meanings in
favour of figurative ones. Thus it is constantly suggested that
there is a key to the problem of interpretation — that it is an
open secret perhaps to those who possess it, but an insoluble
puzzle to those without it. This is a theme begun and nurtured
with Jesus' own exposition of the scriptures, both publicly in
the synagogues and privately with the chosen disciples. It is
continued after his death in Stephen's speech to the Jewish
council, and the subsequent approach to the Gentiles in such
incidents as Philip and the Ethiopian, and Paul preaching of
the 'unknown god' in Athens (Acts 8:26–39, and 17:16–34).
The debate over the exact nature of this 'messianic secret' does
not concern us here; what is significant for our study of the
Bible in its context of world literature is that such a 'secret'
was assumed to exist and to have shaped the structure of the
whole. As we have suggested, it was to have a profound effect
on the subsequent development of European narrative.

To illustrate this we must separate the related but distinct
terms of 'chronicle', 'narrative', and 'history'. A 'chronicle'
is a simple record of a sequence of events as they were perceived or reported to have happened. Though a sophisticated or
sceptical redactor may attempt to assess the reliability of the
sources in question, we do not expect that he will try to shape the
sequence into a story, or draw from it a moral, or judge if the context of the reported events affects our understanding of them. A
'narrative', on the other hand, is specifically concerned to tell

a story. It shapes and selects its material to make its point with maximum effectiveness and is conventionally, if not invariably, structured with a beginning, a middle, and an end. It is concerned with meaning rather than with historical factuality — though, of course, that meaning may itself involve a claim to factuality.

'History', however, involves something of both the previous terms. Its material is that of the chronicle — a record of events as they were believed actually to have happened — but fundamental to it is the search for meaning in the events it recounts. As we have seen, the emerging and distinctive Judeo-Christian sense of 'history' began with the need to explain a problem. The solution was to read back into the Hebrew scriptures the messianic 'secret' of the New Testament, and to show how, with the aid of this guiding principle, everything that went before could be rearranged into a new and coherently organized pattern. It was only in the light of the ending that the earlier events could be seen in their true significance. Though such a pattern was not unique to the Jewish tradition (it is to be found, for instance, in the *Oresteia* of Aeschylus), the re-interpretative ending, with the prestige of the Bible behind it, becomes one of the standard forms of European literature.

Literal and allegorical interpretations

It is hardly surprising, therefore, that the interpretative tradition that grew up around the Bible, from the days of the Church Fathers onwards, centred upon the existence of the Bible not merely as a book, but as *the* Book. For medieval writers it was God who was the supreme author. Indeed, the Latin word for 'author', *auctor*, had been believed by medieval grammarians to contain among its root meanings the verbs *agere* (to perform), and *augere* (to make grow) and the noun *auctoritas* (authority). God, they believed, had not merely created all things, but was the source of all words as well (A. J. Minnis, *Medieval Theory of Authorship*, London, 1984, p. 10). Every human piece of writing stemmed ultimately from the divinely inspired word, the Bible — where God had written down the whole history of the world and, specifically, of mankind, from the first day of Creation to the Last Judgement. Scriptural history was to be understood, therefore, not merely at its face value, but also, like the works of nature, as having a sacramental value. Every event narrated in the Bible was held to have both a literal historical meaning and a spiritual meaning — to be interpreted by means of an ever more elaborate system of allegory and, in particular, by the form known as 'typology'.

Such systems of interpretation were much older than the Middle Ages. As we have seen, even by New Testament times they had already become part of the accepted mental 'set' of the day, and when the early Christians were faced with the problem of re-interpreting the Jewish Scriptures in the light of their own experience, they followed a quite normal and traditional procedure in disclosing the messianic 'secret'. Thus, just as Moses put a veil over his face after he had seen God, to prevent the children of Israel seeing his shining face (Exodus 34: 33–5), so Paul views the Old Testament as containing secrets hitherto veiled from its readers: 'for to this day, when they read the old covenant, that same veil remains unlifted, because only through Christ is it taken away' (II Corinthians 3:14). For Tertullian (*c.* 160–225 AD), the fact that Moses renamed Oshea, the son of Nun, Joshua, which in Hebrew is the same word as Jesus, is a clear piece of typology. Since it was Joshua, not Moses, who led Israel into the Promised Land, this event was to be seen as prefiguring Christ's leading his people, the Church, out of the desert of sin into the eternal life of the land flowing with milk and honey, not through the discipline of the Law of Moses, but through the grace of the Gospel (Erich Auerbach, 'Figura', trans. R. Manheim, in *Scenes from the Drama of European Literature*, New York, 1959, p. 28). To use the correct terminology, Joshua was the 'type', Christ the 'antitype'. By similar typological means, over the next 1000 years innumerable commentators made almost every event of the Old Testament prefigure its antitype in the life of Jesus, or in the life of the early Church.

The importance of this method of biblical interpretation for the subsequent development of European literature and criticism can scarcely be overestimated. From the time of the early Church until almost the end of the eighteenth century, the literal meaning of the Bible was never more than one among many ways of understanding it. Not merely did allegorical, figural, and typological modes of reading co-exist with the literal one, they were often in practice (if not in theory) accorded higher status. Since the Bible was the model for all secular literature, such ways of reading naturally became the model for the way in which all books were to be read. The allegorical levels of *The Divine Comedy* or *The Romance of the Rose* are not in any way optional additions to the basic story; they are a normal and integral part of what literature was expected to be. To put it another way: the idea of an exclusively literal meaning in a text is an essentially modern one — dating, in effect, from the rise of the prose novel in the eighteenth century.

This is not, of course, to suggest that allegorical and typological readings of the Bible remained constant over 1700 years, or that there was general agreement among commentators about the exact meaning of the texts, or even that there was agreement over the number of interpretative levels to be found. Extreme exponents argued for as many as twelve; the Alexandrian school favoured no less than seven; more common was the belief that there were four. This, for instance, was the view of Dante, who, because he assumed it of scripture, also deliberately and explicitly created four similar levels in his *Divine Comedy*, which, though it is of course a religious poem, was never thought of as having the status of anything more than ordinary secular literature. According to John Cassian (c. 360–435), the four levels or senses of scripture are: the literal (or historical) sense, the allegorical, the tropological (or moral), and the anagogical. He cites as an example the figure of Jerusalem (Minnis, *Medieval Theory of Authorship*, p. 34). Historically it is the earthly city, capital of the ancient kingdom of Israel, etc.; allegorically, however, it signifies the Church; tropologically it stands for the souls of all faithful Christians; while anagogically (that is, in its mystical spiritual meaning),

it is the heavenly city of God. A later popular Latin rhyme sum-
marized these senses thus:

> Littera gesta docet, quid credas allegoria,
> Moralis quid agas, quo tendas anagogia.

The letter teaches what happened, the allegorical what to believe,
The moral what to do, the anagogical toward what to aspire.

It is important to realize that the word 'allegory' (Greek
allegoria), as used by biblical exegetes, did not simply convey
the normal classical sense of a fictional story with an inner
meaning – the sense in which Aesop's Fables, for instance,
are often allegorical. Early Christian and medieval commentators use it primarily in a 'figural' sense: that is, because the
people and incidents described were real historical figures, what
they can be made to stand for shares in that reality. The one
guarantees the other. Neither level is in any sense fictional. As
Auerbach puts it, '*Figura* is something real and historical which
announces something else that is also real and historical . . .
Real historical figures are to be interpreted spiritually . . . ,
but the interpretation points to a carnal, hence historical, fulfilment – for truth has become history in flesh' ('Figura', pp.
29, 39).

The Reformation

The controversies of the Reformation did not, to begin with,
constitute a break with the critical methods of the medieval
period, so much as an extension of them. Biblical commentators had always seen their work as much more than simply
a study of critical modes. Contrariwise, it must be remembered
that the Reformation, whatever its political and ecclesiastical
sub-text, arose primarily from a dispute over the meaning of
the Bible. It was not, as it is sometimes presented today, a conflict between authority and individual freedom, but one between two equally dogmatic kinds of authority. For Luther and
Calvin, as for Wyclif and Tyndale, the question was whether
authority resided with the interpretative tradition of the
Catholic Church, or with the text of holy scripture itself. For

those Protestants who believed the latter, the corollary was that, properly understood, the scriptures would provide their own secure interpretation. If in practice Calvin's Geneva was even less tolerant of dissent than Catholicism, it was not least because the written text of the Bible, interpreted within a primarily legal framework of thought, seemed an even surer basis for confidence. Anglicanism, with its uncertain political foundation, might be more ambiguous, but it was scarcely more tolerant. As we shall see, the English Authorized Version of 1611, which seems to reflect such magisterial status and authority, was in fact born from a context of extreme controversy and instability. Some, even then, declared the plain literal meaning to be the only permissible one, but for others, faced with, in effect, the same problem of legitimacy that had beset the early Church, the traditional modes of allegorical exegesis were to provide sufficient ammunition. In defending their case, Protestant exegetes were quick to show how the Reformation was itself a 'biblical' event that was similarly implicit both in the historical events leading to it and in the prophecies of the Bible itself. Thus Rome could be identified with prophecies in Daniel and Revelation, and phrases like the 'whore of Babylon' and the 'Scarlet Woman' passed into the standard rhetoric of religious and political abuse. For Catholic and Protestant sides alike, the question of biblical interpretation was less an academic study than a matter of life and death. Tyndale himself was burned at the stake − mercifully after having been first strangled. Hundreds died in England, thousands in France, millions in Germany and central Europe.

The re-centring of authority on the text of the Bible itself was intimately bound up with questions of translation. In what sense could the text be held to be inspired? Was the Latin Vulgate the sole authoritative text, or was the Bible to be available in the vernacular − with the uncomfortable corollary that hermeneutics might be brought into the realm of popular debate? Given the political and social consequences that might now depend upon them, the actual words of scripture acquired, if possible, even greater importance. Moreover, as the Reformers were quick to point out, behind the Latin of

Jerome's Vulgate were older and therefore self-evidently more accurate Hebrew and Greek texts. Thus the series of Protestant English translations that culminated in the Authorized Version was matched by Catholic English translations of both Old and New Testaments, known from their places of printing in France as the Rheims and Douai Bibles respectively.

Under such conditions the injunction to 'search the scriptures' took on a new urgency – upon it after all might depend the individual's salvation. Indeed, it was not enough to 'search'; to be certain one had to 'make trial' of them – interrogate them in an almost legal sense to make them yield up their sacred treasures. David Knowles, in his study of the Reformation in England, has called attention to the astonishing ascendancy of lawyers in English society at the beginning of the sixteenth century (*Bare Ruined Choirs,* Cambridge, 1976, pp. 4–60). Thomas More was recalled by his father from the useless humanism of Oxford and made to study law. Aske, Cromwell, Audley, Rich, Layton, Legh, and Sir Thomas Eliot, like Calvin in Geneva, all had legal backgrounds. A hundred years later, Milton's Samson, eyeless in Gaza and questioning in agony the prophecies on which his life has hitherto been based, so far from being guilty of impiety, is in fact displaying impeccable Protestant credentials – echoing from his own symbolic blindness the no less desperate cross-questionings of the earlier Catholic Renaissance humanists.

Enlightenment and Romantic criticism

Biblical interpretation was always a pluralistic affair, and we should be on guard against simple-minded periodization. Different and even incompatible modes of thinking could and often did overlap. As we shall see, essentially medieval modes of typology were to last until well into the nineteenth century, and what we think of as the nineteenth-century conception of historical criticism has roots as far back as the seventeenth. In 1678, a French Oratorian, Richard Simon, had published his *Histoire critique du Vieux Testament.* To counter the Protestant principle that scripture alone was necessary for salvation, Simon, by applying the kind of scholarly techniques then being developed for classical texts, set out to show that the origins of biblical texts were complex, and that careful guidance (from the Church, naturally) was necessary to understand their meaning. He rapidly challenged the traditional view that Moses was the author of the Pentateuch, and suggested that these books were more likely to be the composite creation of scribes and 'public writers' (Françoise Deconinck-Brossard in *Reading the Text: Biblical Interpretation and Literary Theory*, ed. Stephen Prickett, Oxford, 1991). Ironically, such suggestions aroused the immediate wrath of the Catholic hierarchy in France, and the book was banned. A few copies were, however, smuggled to England. A translation followed as early as 1682, and it was from England that the next developments in biblical criticism were to come.

In fact, England gave Simon's *Critical History of the Old Testament* a mixed reception. Edward Stillingfleet, for instance, the Dean of St Paul's and later Bishop of Worcester, attacked it as undermining the authority of scripture. Locke and Dryden, however, were both deeply impressed by it, and its influence was widespread enough in the eighteenth-century controversies over Deism to pave the way for the next major work in the history of biblical criticism, Robert Lowth's *Sacred Poetry of the Hebrews*, which was first published (in Latin) in 1753, but not fully translated into English until 1778.

Lowth was elected to the Chair of Poetry at Oxford in May 1741, and found himself with the unenviable prospect of having to begin his series of lectures almost at once, with almost no time to prepare by consulting the usual academic sources. Being an able theologian and Hebrew scholar, he seems to have turned initially to his theme of biblical poetry more to save time than because he intended to say anything revolutionary. Nevertheless, for an age still accustomed to typological and figural interpretations, Lowth's avowed aim in the first lecture struck a quite new note:

He who would perceive the peculiar and interior elegancies of the Hebrew poetry, must imagine himself exactly situated as the persons for whom it was written, or even as the writers themselves; he is to feel them as a Hebrew . . . nor is it enough to be acquainted with the language of this people, their manners, discipline, rites and ceremonies; we must even investigate their inmost sentiments, the manner and connexion of their thoughts; in one word, we must see all things with their eyes, estimate all things by their opinion: we must endeavour as much as possible to read Hebrew as the Hebrews would have done it.   (Vol. I, pp. 113f)

This is not, of course, the same emphasis as Simon's. Whereas the French Catholic was interested primarily in the accuracy of the texts that have come down to us, the Oxford professor was more interested in the context from which those documents arose. Nevertheless, the latter presupposes the former: from a study of the original Hebrew texts of the Bible a new (and essentially modern) idea of history is beginning to emerge. Instead of trying to piece together the four- (seven- or twelve-) fold meanings divinely encoded within the scriptures, Lowth is trying to re-create, if not the intentions of the biblical writers, at least their state of mind as human beings in a social framework. The result was two major breakthroughs in critical theory, both of which were to affect the whole development of English poetry.

The first was the identification of the Old Testament concepts of prophecy and poetry. The Hebrew word 'Nabi', explains Lowth, was used to mean 'a prophet, a poet, or a musician, under the influence of divine inspiration'. The prophets of ancient Israel were, he argued, a kind of professional caste, trained both 'to compose verses for the service of the church, and to declare the oracles of God'. Similarly, 'Mashal', one of the words commonly used for a poem in Hebrew, is also the word translated in the New Testament as 'parable'. In other words, the parables of Jesus, so far from being an innovation, were an extension, by the greatest of the biblical 'poets', of the basic forms of the Hebrew prophetic tradition.

From this followed a second, technical, discovery: the secret of the construction of Hebrew verse itself. Whereas all European poetry had depended upon such aural techniques as rhyme, rhythm and alliteration, no such techniques could be discovered in Hebrew verse − not even in the Psalms, which were clearly intended to be songs. Even among eighteenth-century Jews the art of Hebrew poetry had been completely lost. Lowth was now able to demonstrate in his lectures that in fact Hebrew poetry was constructed upon quite different principles from European, and depended primarily upon a feature which he called 'parallelism':

The Correspondence of one verse, or line, with another, I call parallelism. When a proposition is delivered, and a second subjoined to it, or drawn under it, equivalent, or contrasted with it in sense; or similar to it in the form of grammatical construction; these I call parallel lines; and the words or phrases, answering one to another in the corresponding lines, parallel terms.   (Vol. II, p. 32)

The origins of this form, Lowth argued, like the origins of European poetic forms, lay in the oral tradition − but in this case in the antiphonal chants and choruses we find mentioned in various places in the Old Testament. Lowth cites, for instance, I Samuel 18:7, where David returns victorious from a battle with the Philistines and the women greet him with the chant of 'Saul hath smote his thousands' and are answered by a second chorus with the parallel 'And David his ten thousands' (Vol. II, p. 53). Lowth distinguishes no less than eight different kinds of parallelism, ranging from simple repetition and echo to variation, comparison and contrast − as in the case given above, where the force of the contrast was not lost on Saul, as he promptly tried to have David assassinated.

These discoveries inaugurated a critical revolution. The poet could now justifiably be seen not as an illustrator or decorator of received wisdom, but as a prophet, a transformer of society, and a mediator of divine truth. It is the difference between Blake and Wordsworth (both of whom had absorbed Lowth's work) and, say, Pope. Associated with this was a change in the status of the Bible itself. By and large, in 1700 the principal literary models were classical; by 1800 they were more likely to be biblical. Even as an increasing number of people were calling the literal truth of many of the biblical stories into question, the Bible had supplanted the classics as a model of both naturalness and sublimity. Lowth himself, in the preface to his new translation of Isaiah (1778), had made a comparison with Aristotle's *Poetics*, which he referred to as 'the Great Code of Criticism' (*Isaiah*, Vol. I, p. lxxviii). Blake was at once acknowledging Lowth and challenging him when he wrote in 1821 that 'The Old and New Testaments are the Great Code of Art'. At the heart of Romanticism is a return to what were seen as biblical aesthetics.

Lowth's work had another, less immediately foreseeable, consequence. Because Hebrew poetry relied on parallelism rather than the traditional techniques of European verse, it was, Lowth claimed, best translated into prose: 'a poem translated literally from the Hebrew into the prose of any other language, whilst the same form of the sentences remain, will still retain, even as far as relates to versification, much of its dignity, and a fair appearance of versification' (Vol. I, pp. 71f.). As critics were quick to observe, this meant that, whereas conventional poetry was extremely difficult to translate into another language with any real equivalence of tone and feeling, the Bible was peculiarly, if not uniquely, open to translation. In particular, the majestic prose rhythms of the Authorized Version were, in fact, closer to the original than any attempt at versification would have been. This observation had the unforeseen effect of blurring traditional distinctions between prose and verse. To speak of a prose piece as 'poetic' could now be more than just a metaphor. The result is apparent not merely in Blake, who was steeped in the Bible, but also (though Lowth could hardly have suspected such a consequence) in the shift from verse to prose as the main creative literary medium that took place progressively during the nineteenth century after the rise of the novel.

If the principal effect of Lowth's work in England was literary, in Germany it was more on the development of biblical criticism itself — and, in particular, on the 'higher' critics, such as Michaelis, Reimarus, Lessing, and Eichhorn. So far from being divinely inspired, for them the Bible had to be read as the record of the myths and aspirations of an ancient and primitive Near Eastern tribe. The accounts of God's appearances and other miracles were to be seen as part of a particularly powerful (and, be it said) eclectic mythology. As the French Revolutionary writer C. F. Volney anticipated in his influential book, *The Ruins of Empires* (1792), many of the Genesis stories were discovered to have been borrowed from older Babylonian and other Near Eastern myths, and even from ancient Egypt. What meaning there was in such stories was moral and developmental rather than historical — illustrating what Lessing, in the title of one of his best-known books, called *The Education of the Human Race* (1780). If such narratives were to be given a different status from the myths of, say, Greece or Rome, it was on account of their 'moral beauty', or the profoundly ethical nature of their teachings. Though such arguments were commonplace in Germany and France by the end of the eighteenth century, their introduction into Britain was delayed both by the political backlash against the French Revolution, which was inclined to see such radical criticism of the scriptures as Volney's (translated into English during the 1790s) as being little more than revolutionary Jacobinism, and by the lack of any corresponding native school of biblical critics to pave their way.

Thus, for example, a popular English biblical commentary of the early nineteenth century like Mrs Sarah Trimmer's *Help to the Unlearned in the Study of the Holy Scriptures* (1806) is still as firmly typological as any medieval monk's. The story of Abraham and Isaac (Genesis 22:1–14), for instance, is read primarily as a type of the Crucifixion:

Abraham spoke prophetically, ver. 8, and his words were verified; God did provide himself a lamb. Abraham's offering up his son was a type of GOD's giving his son, our LORD JESUS CHRIST, as a sacrifice for mankind. Mount Moriah, where Abraham offered up Isaac, was the place on which the house of the Lord at Jerusalem was afterwards built. We should learn from Abraham's example to be ready to submit to GOD's will in the most severe trials, and to trust always in his providence.   (pp. 130–1)

This is actually nothing less than a repetition of a standard fourfold reading. The literal sense is too clear to need comment; the allegorical concerns Isaac as the 'lamb' of God — the 'type' of Christ; the identification of Mount Moriah with the site of the later Jerusalem Temple leads us on anagogically to the idea of the Church as founded on the blood of the lamb; while the moral instructs us how we should behave in consequence.

Such was the context in which, in 1840, some six years after Coleridge's death, a collection of his essays was published by his nephew, Henry Nelson Coleridge, under the title *Confessions of an Inquiring Spirit*. The personal connotations of that word 'confessions' were quite deliberate. H. N. Coleridge was treading on dangerous ground. His uncle's original title, *Letters on the Inspiration of the Scriptures*, had been far too descriptively accurate − not to say provocative − for an early Victorian religious public, already shaken by the suggestions of geologists and palaeontologists that the dating of Genesis could not be correct. As so often happens, the effect of the theological furore was to divert attention from certain much more original and important aspects of Coleridge's argument. For him, the Bible was to be read as one might 'any other book', and not to be subject to what he called 'bibliolatry' − the idolizing of individual texts torn loose from their context and used as if they had a freestanding universal meaning. Similarly, its importance was not secured by divine fiat, but rather was something to be discovered by practical and imaginative experience on the part of the reader. In an appendix to *The Statesman's Manual* he described the scriptures, using a term borrowed from the chemistry of the period, as 'the living educts of the imagination' giving 'birth to a system of symbols, harmonious in themselves, and consubstantial with the Truths, of which they are the conductors . . . Hence . . . the Sacred Book is worthily entitled the WORD OF GOD' (1972 edn, pp. 28f).

Coleridge's position was, therefore, somewhat more original − and certainly more important − than his many critics gave him credit for. His insistence on the symbolic value of the biblical narratives as 'the living educts of the imagination' was less a cover for infidelity than an attempt to preserve the traditional many-layered approach to the Bible and base it on something less shaky than the literal meaning ascribed to particular doubtful and translated texts. In this respect, his claim to read it as he might 'any other book' takes on a new significance. He is, in effect, applying a hermeneutic method that is as appropriate to the novel as it is to a sacred text. Indeed, it is not accidental that even as typology, as a mode of biblical interpretation, was under threat from more critical and historical hermeneutics, it was to undergo a revival in the form of symbolism in the new art-form of the novel. To put it another way: the rise in status of the novel, and of prose fiction generally, is closely bound up with the contemporaneous shift in the status of biblical narrative. In both cases, it was increasingly recognized that myth, symbolic narrative, and even transparent fiction (such as, for instance, the Book of Jonah) could convey truths more important than the most scrupulously factual history.

Yet Coleridge's *Confessions* were less the beginning of a new critical era than the end of an old. For various entirely contingent reasons (which had more to do with German academic administration than hermeneutics), the study of the Bible and secular literature became separated from one another early in the nineteenth century. At the very period when literary critics were becoming increasingly sensitive to the symbolic and polysemous nature of narrative, biblical critics were dominated by the most rigid and materialistic notions of history – and fiction.

Biblical criticism

In the later nineteenth century the terms 'lower' and 'higher' criticism began to be applied to biblical study – 'lower' referring to textual criticism, and 'higher' to the study of the sources and literary techniques of the biblical authors. By that time, the German tradition of source analysis of the Pentateuch in particular was becoming known in the English-speaking world, a tradition which reached a sort of fixity in the works of Julius Wellhausen, especially *Die Geschichte Israels* (1878), which appeared in English as *Prolegomena to the History of Ancient Israel* in 1885, and *Die Komposition des Hexateuchs* (1885).

Wellhausen claimed that there were four main literary sources, or strands, in the Pentateuch. The 'J', or 'Yahwistic' source, which used the name 'Yahweh' for God almost from the beginning of Genesis, and which he believed was the earliest history of Israel, starting from the creation, was composed in the early Israelite monarchy. The 'E', or 'Elohistic' source, which used the name 'Elohim' for God, especially for the period before the revelation of the name 'Yahweh' to Moses at Sinai, was a slightly later history of Israel, composed in the northern kingdom of Israel, and only combined with J after the fall of that kingdom to the Assyrians. The 'D', or 'Deuteronomistic' source, essentially the Book of Deuteronomy, was composed in the late monarchy. The 'P', or 'Priestly' source, the latest of all, came from the time of the exile and after, and was an amalgamation of the other sources with much further material, both narrative and legal.

This 'four-source' analysis of the Pentateuch has been widely accepted by biblical scholars, but has also attracted criticism of various kinds: it was incompatible with the traditional Jewish and Christian belief that Moses wrote the Pentateuch under immediate divine inspiration; it seemed to put great weight on the different names used for God, which might be explained in other ways, and it seemed to some an excessively bookish view of Israelite history writing, assuming an early literary tradition in Israel and synthetic methods of composition that might be quite inappropriate for the period. Nevertheless, it was Wellhausen's source-analysis of the Pentateuch above all which gave 'biblical criticism' both its basic scholarly methods and its occasional public notoriety.

The twentieth century's most significant addition to the Wellhausen tradition has probably been form criticism. At the turn of the century Hermann Gunkel produced a commentary on Genesis, as well as a more popular book which appeared in English as *The Legends of Genesis* in 1901. In some ways, both were a reaction against Wellhausen. Gunkel maintained that the stories of the patriarchs, Abraham, Isaac, and Jacob, were ancient sagas, similar to other popular tribal and family stories in the ancient Near East, which had had a long oral tradition before they were written down. To appreciate them correctly, the reader had to discern their original 'setting in life' (the German term *Sitz im Leben* is still often used), as well as any modifications they may have undergone when written down as part of a larger, literary history. These sagas were not history in the modern sense of the term, though they might give some indication to modern historians of the social conditions of their period of origin. Gunkel later also wrote a highly influential commentary on the Psalms, which grouped them into such categories as 'hymn', 'communal lament', 'individual lament', 'individual thanksgiving', 'royal psalm', etc.; this assumes that the Psalms too had a 'setting in life', in the Israelite cult, which can be discerned behind their present literary form. Much further work has since been devoted to the possible cultic setting of the Psalms, with scholars claiming varying degrees of similarity between them and other cultic poetry of the ancient Near East.

In New Testament studies, 'form criticism' has been applied particularly to the Synoptic Gospels. Rudolf Bultmann, in *The History of the Synoptic Tradition* (1963; German original 1921), analysed the Synoptic material into such earlier elements of the Jesus tradition as apothegms (stories that lead up to some remarkable saying), prophetic and apocalyptic sayings, proverbs, wisdom sayings, community rules, legends, miracle stories, exorcisms, healings, tales, and so on. He assumed that these earlier units had been handed down orally before they were written into the Gospels, and that a careful reader could discern their earlier 'setting in life' (particularly if that reader studied comparable material from elsewhere in the Jewish tradition and the Greco-Roman world, of which Bultmann supplied many fascinating examples). Bultmann himself claimed that, in dealing with the Jesus tradition, what we can discern is much more the material's 'setting in the life of the church' than its 'setting in the life of Jesus'; in other words, the oral transmission of the material by the Church, in all sorts of preaching and apologetic situations, has made it impossible to recover much authentic information about Jesus. This last claim appears to some more recent scholars as excessive, and perhaps unduly influenced by Bultmann's evident desire to exclude any sort of reliance by Christians on historical facts rather than faith. It should be added, however, that Bultmann's work on the Synoptic tradition, the problem of history and faith, the sources and composition of John, and the theology of Paul and the rest of the New Testament has set more of the agenda for critical twentieth-century New Testament study than the work of any other scholar.

It should also be added that the tradition of biblical criticism has itself recently developed new techniques, which are highly relevant to any literary criticism of the Bible. These include 'redaction criticism', which studies the way in which the 'final' author has redacted or edited his material, and in particular examines any theological concerns that his editing manifests; there have been some especially notable studies of the Synoptic Gospels along these lines. Another, but perhaps more controversial, technique is 'canonical criticism', which examines not merely the books of the Bible in their 'final', canonical form, but in particular considers them as parts of a canon of scripture which is sacred to Jewish and/or Christian religious communities.

Modern hermeneutics

In spite of the growing rift between the study of the Bible and the study of secular literature in the nineteenth century, referred to above, there have been some signs that the gap might be bridged in the late twentieth century. This is partly an aspect of the secularization of western societies: as most members of those societies have gradually lost interest in the Bible as a 'sacred' book (and indeed have very largely lost interest in it altogether), it has at last become possible to consider it as a work of literature. The recovery of substantial fragments of other ancient Near Eastern literatures has, on the one hand, stripped the Bible of the unique status which it once enjoyed, but on the other made its real literary distinctiveness much clearer. The various kinds of biblical criticism, mentioned above, may have seemed to 'tear the Bible apart', and give excessive attention to its basic units rather than its final form, but they have certainly made us more conscious of the Bible as a written text. Finally, modern hermeneutical theory, especially as developed in Germany and France, may now help to clarify for us both the whole question of human understanding of texts and the historical emergence of different narrative forms – including, of course, the forms of our basic book, the Bible.

Hermeneutical theory in its modern continental form is more than merely a study of how one culture understands another. A recent textbook, edited by Kurt Mueller-Vollmer, *The Hermeneutics Reader: Texts of the German Tradition from the Enlightenment to the Present* (New York, 1985), includes an outline history of this tradition, as well as some typical readings. Mueller-Vollmer rightly sees the German Romantic theologian Friedrich Schleiermacher as the watershed in the development of modern hermeneutics. Schleiermacher, following Kant, gave hermeneutics a 'transcendental' turn: the problem was not to decode a given meaning in a text, but to grasp how any human understanding of a text, or any other human cultural product, was possible. In fact, he believed, all understanding derived from man's capacity for speech, which is realized by each person acquiring a particular language at a particular historical time. This means that, whenever a person understands a text, two quite separate things are involved: the person's grasp of the interpersonal language in which the text is expressed, and his or her own internal or mental history. It follows that no text has a fixed meaning, intended by the author: all texts (and indeed all human utterances) have a kind of fluid and dynamic existence, which is apprehended somewhat differently each time they are read or heard by a particular individual. Further, as Schleiermacher put it, 'the innate nature of language modifies our mind'.

Modern German hermeneutic theory, as presented by Mueller-Vollmer, is essentially a development of Schleiermacher's insights. One key later notion in this tradition is that of the 'hermeneutic circle'. No single sentence of, say, a historical text has any immediate meaning. The historian begins his writing by assuming some coherence and meaning in the whole story he will tell, though of course the process of writing may modify the coherence and meaning he originally assumed. Similarly, the reader of his history starts with certain assumptions about what this story will mean, but his assumptions too will be modified as he reads on. Both thus begin from a complete 'circle' of assumed meaning, and then add the segments to make up this circle, though by the time they finish it is likely to be a rather different circle. Such lines of thought were extensively considered around the turn of the twentieth century by the philosopher Wilhelm Dilthey, who was particularly concerned to grasp the proper methodology for the human sciences (above all, history writing and reading), as distinct from the natural sciences. Dilthey maintained that the enormous intellectual prestige of the natural sciences in modern times had imposed quite unrealistic 'scientific' methodologies on such human sciences as history. All human historical sources are essentially the 'life-expressions' of the individuals who created them, and they can only be apprehended in later times by something very like intuition, or imagination. The historian interprets those sources according to, and as part of, his own life-expression; and the reader of his history does the same according to, and as part of, *his* life-expressions.

One of the most influential recent thinkers on hermeneutics is Hans-Georg Gadamer, who is particularly concerned not only with how the individual reader apprehends a text, but with how the readers of a text in any particular age contribute to a tradition of interpretation of the text. He writes:

The [hermeneutic] circle, then, is not formal in nature, it is neither subjective nor objective, but describes understanding as the interplay of the movement of tradition and the movement of the interpreter. The anticipation of meaning that governs our understanding of a text is not an act of subjectivity, but proceeds from the communality that binds us to the tradition . . . Thus the meaning of the connection with tradition, i.e. the element of tradition in our historical, hermeneutical attitude, is fulfilled in the fact that we share fundamental prejudices with tradition . . . Every age has to understand a transmitted text in its own way, for the text is part of the whole of the tradition in which the age takes an objective interest and in which it seeks to understand itself. The real meaning of a text, as it speaks to the interpreter, does not depend on the contingencies of the author and whom he originally wrote for. It is certainly not identical with them, for it is always partly determined also by the historical situation of the interpreter and hence by the totality of the objective course of history.

(*Truth and Method*, New York, 1975, pp. 261–3)

By means of the 'prejudices' that we share with the tradition, the 'strangeness' of the historical sources is overcome, and their 'horizon' is assimilated to our own. However, both the sources and their interpreter then become united as parts of a cultural tradition or continuum, which Gadamer calls 'effective history'.

It is not hard to see the relevance of hermeneutic theory to our understanding of the Bible. According to such theory, the Bible will be essentially a product of human cultural development at particular times and places, rather than, say, the product of direct inspiration from a God who is believed to stand outside human cultural evolution. Further, it will not have any fixed meaning, or any fixed canon or order of its parts. As long as it continues to be read at all, and thus remains part of our 'effective history', its 'horizons' will be assimilated in very various ways to those of its readers and hearers.

The Bible as 'history-likeness'

What many of these interpretative theories of the last 200 years have in common is the argument that the Bible is primarily to be seen as 'literature', to be set against other works of literature. Behind them lies the late eighteenth-century crisis over the historicity of the biblical records and the desire to find some other category by which the Bible's perceived religious value might be defended. One distinguished student of this trend is the historian of biblical interpretation Hans Frei, who has suggested that, so far from trying to regard biblical narrative as history in the sense aimed for by Leopold von Ranke (i.e. narrating the events of the past 'as they actually happened') and so having to think of it in terms of factual or non-factual, we should rather think of it as, in his words, 'fact-like' (*The*

Eclipse of Biblical Narrative: A Study in Eighteenth and Nine-
teenth Century Hermeneutics, New Haven, Connecticut, 1974).
That is, instead of attempting to see it as history − an attempt
in his opinion foredoomed to failure − we should rather try
to understand it in terms of realistic prose fiction − on the
lines, perhaps, of the nineteenth-century realistic novel. As we
all know, a fictional story may in some sense be more 'true'
of a situation, an experience, or a society than any description
of an actual event. We should not ask of it, therefore: did this
actually happen to real people? but: is this 'true to life', is this
artistically true? If, as some have argued, such a position was
implicit in Coleridge, it has certainly been explicit in England
ever since Matthew Arnold's *Literature and Dogma* (1873), and
it has gained wide support in the past 100 years. For all their
individual emphases and differences − which should not
be minimized − such an approach to biblical narrative is
broadly common not merely to Frei, and to Robert Funk, but
to philosophers like Paul Ricoeur, as well as to such literary
biblical commentators as Northrop Frye and Robert Alter.

Yet such an approach has its own dangers. The grosser
absurdities of the factual−non-factual dichotomy − advanc-
ed in this case by a British follower of Bultmann − were sharply ridiculed by C. S. Lewis:

I read that the fourth Gospel is regarded by one school as a 'spiritual
romance', 'a poem not a history', to be judged by the same canons
as Nathan's parable, the book of Jonah, Paradise Lost, 'or, more
exactly, Pilgrim's Progress'. After a man has said that, why need we
attend to anything else he says about any book in the world? Note
that he regards Pilgrim's Progress, a story which professes to be a
dream and flaunts its allegorical nature by every single proper name
it uses, as the closest parallel. Note that the whole epic panoply of
Milton goes for nothing. But even if we leave out the grosser absurdities and keep to Jonah, the insensitiveness is crass − Jonah, a tale
with as few even pretended historical attachments as Job, grotesque
in incident and surely not without a distinct . . . vein of typically Jewish
humour. Then turn to John. Read the dialogues: that with the
Samaritan woman at the well, or that which follows the healing of
the man born blind. Look at its pictures: Jesus . . . doodling with
his fingers in the dust . . . I have been reading poems, romances, vision-
literature, legends, myths all my life. I know that not one of

them is like this. Of this text there are only two possible views. Either this is reportage – though it may no doubt contain errors – pretty close up to the facts; nearly as close as Boswell. Or else, some unknown writer in the second century, without known predecessors or successors, suddenly anticipated the technique of modern, novelistic, realistic narrative. If it is untrue, it must be narrative of that kind. The reader who doesn't see this has simply not learned to read. I would recommend him to read Auerbach.

(*Fern-Seeds and Elephants*, London, 1975, pp. 107–8).

The literary crassness of the commentator in question is fair game, but Lewis is also making a much shrewder point about the nature of 'realism' itself. The kind of 'fact-like fiction' being pre-supposed by Frei and Alter violates everything that we know about the history of literary genres and begs the question of the nature of the categories of history and literature in a way that is itself curiously un-historical. What a nineteenth-century novelist might call 'realism', or Frei 'history-likeness', is *itself* culturally variable. David Lodge, for instance, in a discussion of the nature of realism, has suggested that it is best defined in relative terms as: 'the representation of experience in a manner which approximates closely to descriptions of similar experience in a nonliterary text of the same culture' (*Modes of Modern Writing*, London, 1977). Such a definition works excellently for the nineteenth century, when the concept of literary realism was invented. But if we take the example of a non-literary prose text from a pre-scientific era, say from Gregory of Tours in the sixth century AD, it contains as a matter of course all manner of miraculous events not so easily found in Europe 1300 years later. Here the miraculous and magical would have to be the basis of realism. There is, in fact, a nice example of this paradox if we compare two historical novels about the early Church, by Charles Kingsley and John Henry Newman. Newman's novel *Callista* concludes with some miracles worked by that fictitious lady's remains after her death, when she is venerated as a Christian martyr. It is, therefore, by this definition highly realistic, whereas Kingsley's novel, *Hypatia*, which is written for the most part to the best canons of nineteenth-century realism, clearly does not qualify.

When we turn to biblical narrative itself, this problem is compounded. Whereas we can compare, say, a novel by George Eliot with other non-literary texts of the same culture in order to judge its realism, there is no way we can do this with II Kings, or Mark's Gospel. It is not just that what histories we do have (Josephus, for instance) are inadequate to form the basis for comparison. In a world like that of the Old Testament, where every event, from the rising of the sun each morning to Elijah's assumption to Heaven in a fiery chariot, exists at the same plane of causal explanation — which can neither be thought of as 'naturalistic' nor as 'miraculous' in our senses — 'realism' of our kind is not a possible concept. It could only appear for the first time with the post-Rankean concept of history in the nineteenth century. Because it presupposes the existence of a secular, objective, and non-miraculous mode of thought, 'realism' or 'history-likeness' as a fictional technique has little place in the Bible (an argument that does not apply, of course, to the possibility raised by Lewis of straight reporting).

Contrariwise, if what we mean by history turns out to be no more than a particular form of narrative, purporting to be an actual record of events, that conforms to the criteria for credibility in that particular society, then II Kings is surely perfectly good history. Our hermeneutic problem has not, of course, gone away: it has simply been transposed into a problem of narrative. Yet much of the current debate over the historicity of the Bible unwittingly puts the cart before the horse precisely when it considers narrative, since, as we have seen, our concept of narrative, as distinct from chronicle, was initially derived *from* the Bible itself. Most critics would now accept that our categories of history, myth, and fiction are all constructs by which we attempt to make sense of our past. But to describe the Bible in any of these terms is highly misleading. It belongs, as we have seen, to a period when such essentially modern distinctions did not and could not yet exist; and in attempting to apply such models to it, we should always be conscious of what we *lose* in our reading of the original. As we shall see in connection with the history of biblical translation in chapter 5, the degree to which modern translators have been guided by these categories has had profound, if not always conscious, effects on the way they have gone about their task.

Chapter 5

The Bible and literature

Translation within the biblical tradition

As pointed out earlier, the Bible was from the first a palimpsest of languages and contexts. The Hebrew Bible did not evolve in a cultural vacuum, but as a sort of translation from and commentary (often in highly critical terms) upon the older literatures of Mesopotamia, Egypt, Canaan, and other parts of the Near East. After the return from the exile at the latest, it became necessary to follow readings from the Hebrew text with an 'interpretation' in Aramaic (this seems to be the point of Ezra 8:8), and from about the third century BC on these Aramaic 'Targums' came to be written down in continuous form. The surviving manuscripts of the Targums were transcribed between the seventh and the sixteenth centuries AD and certainly include some very late elements, but most scholars believe that they give a good general impression of Jewish understanding of the Bible at about the time of Jesus, if not much earlier. To get some idea of their importance, compare the following passage from a Targum of Isaiah 53 with any translation of the Hebrew:

Who has believed these tidings of ours, and to whom has the power of the mighty arm of the Lord been revealed? And the righteous will grow up before him like budding shoots; and as a tree that sends forth its roots by streams of water, so will the holy generations increase in the land that needed him: his appearance will not be that of a common man, nor the fear of him that of an ordinary man; but his countenance will be a holy countenance, so that all who see him will regard him earnestly. Then will the glory of the kingdoms be despised and come to an end; they will be infirm and sick like a man of sorrows and one destined for sicknesses, and as when the presence of the Shekinah [i.e. God's 'dwelling' with Israel] was withdrawn from us, they will be despised and of no account. Then he will pray on behalf of our transgressions, and our sins will be pardoned for his sake, though we were accounted smitten, stricken before the Lord, and afflicted. But he will build the sanctuary that was polluted because of our transgressions, and given up because of our sins . . . He was praying, and he was answered, and before he opened his mouth he was accepted; the mighty ones of the people he will deliver up like a lamb to the slaughter . . . Out of chastisements and out of punishment he will bring our exiles near . . . He will take away the dominion of the peoples from the land of Israel, and the sins which my people sinned he will transfer to them . . . And it was the Lord's good pleasure to refine and purify the remnant of his people, in order to cleanse their souls from sin; they will look upon the kingdoms of their Messiah. . .

(J. F. Stenning, *The Targum of Isaiah,* Oxford, 1949,
translation modified)

We see at once that the 'Suffering Servant' of Isaiah 53 has been identified with the Messiah in the Targum, but that any suggestion of the Messiah having to suffer has been excluded, to the extent of doing violence to the obvious meaning of the Hebrew; all the suffering will now be inflicted on the Gentiles. This passage apparently means that, at the time of Jesus, there was *no* idea in Judaism that the Messiah should suffer, in which case Jesus' claim that he himself 'must suffer many things . . . and be killed' (Mark 8:31) becomes all the more startling, and Peter's 'rebuke' to him for saying it all the more understandable. New Testament scholars are coming to see that, in this and very many other passages, the New Testament is assuming, or reading against, not so much the Hebrew Bible, as the interpretation of the Bible that we see in the Aramaic Targums. Major themes of the fourth Gospel, for example, such as the Word of God who becomes flesh, the glory of the Lord, the bread from heaven, and the Lamb of God, almost certainly presuppose such Targumic interpretations.

Much the same can be said of the Septuagint, or Greek translation of the Hebrew Bible. According to a story recounted in the 'Letter of Aristeas', this translation (or at least the translation of the Pentateuch) was made in the third century BC at the request of King Ptolemy II Philadelphus of Egypt, who sent to Jerusalem for 'seventy' (actually seventy-two) translators, and they carried it out in seventy-two days, with their different attempts being found to agree perfectly with each other. The story seems concerned to show that the translation was carried out under proper Jewish auspices, and with miraculous fidelity. In fact, the translation seems much more piecemeal than this suggests, with different styles and translation techniques in different parts, and it may well have taken several centuries to reach its present form. It is, however, a vital element in the whole ancient Bible tradition, partly because it is translated from forms of the Hebrew Bible much older than the surviving complete Hebrew manuscripts; partly because it became the normal Bible in the Hellenistic world, and therefore of the early Christian church; and partly because it includes the Apocrypha, rejected from the Hebrew Bible, but still important sources for Jewish culture in the 'inter-testamental' period. As a reliable translation from the Hebrew, it varies in quality, and several revisions of it in the early centuries AD tried to make it follow the Hebrew more literally.

Very frequently the New Testament quotes the Bible according to the Septuagint rather than the Hebrew meaning (where the two differ). One famous case of this is at Matthew 1:23, where Isaiah 7:14 is quoted in the Septuagint form: 'Behold, a virgin shall conceive and bear a son . . .', rather than the Hebrew 'young woman'. Almost certainly, too, the tendency for Christian interpreters of the Bible to find Christ 'present' in the Old Testament was facilitated by the regular Septuagint translation *ho Kyrios* ('the Lord', which had become a normal title for Jesus) for the Hebrew 'Yahweh' (Jews of course regularly substituted 'Adonai', 'the Lord', for this, but they were always aware that this was a substitution, whereas Christian Greek readers would be likely to believe that their 'Lord', Jesus, was actually being referred to in the Old Testament).

The Vulgate

The term 'Vulgate', or 'common', version usually refers to Jerome's revision of earlier Latin versions of the whole Bible, which he began in 382 AD. His revision eventually prevailed as the normal Bible of Western Christianity down to the time of the Reformation, and in the Roman Catholic Church until much more recently. Jerome was, for his day, a good Hebrew and Greek scholar, but, as with the Septuagint translation of the Hebrew, his reliability varies. One of his renderings, which was to be attacked at the Reformation, was of the words of John the Baptist at Matthew 3:2. The Greek reads 'Repent, for the kingdom of heaven is at hand', for which Jerome gave: 'Penitentiam agite, adpropinquavit enim regnum caelorum', which the Reformers believed gave an unwarranted authority to the Catholic sacrament of penance. His rendering of Romans 5:12 has also created problems: the Greek almost certainly means 'Therefore as sin came into the world through one man and death through sin, and so death spread to all men because [or perhaps better 'inasmuch as'] all men sinned . . .' (RSV), but Jerome rendered the last phrase as 'in quo omnes peccaverunt', which might be taken to mean 'in whom (i.e. Adam) all men sinned', and therefore as a justification of the doctrine of 'original sin'.

Jerome (like his contemporary Augustine) was highly trained in the classical Latin rhetorical tradition, and therefore tended to regard the literary styles of the Bible with some disdain. His translation of the Bible has its own rather haunting cadences, but it does not reflect much sensitivity to the structure and imagery of Hebrew poetry, and is sometimes meaningless (the same might be said of the Authorized Version in places). He (again like Augustine) thought that the Bible's 'humble' style and 'obscurity' were intended by God to make its readers look deeper than its surface meaning. As the European vernaculars gradually diverged from Latin during the Dark Ages, and education in Latin came to be almost restricted to the clergy, this 'obscurity' became ever darker to most Christians. For them, the Bible could only be 'read' through the liturgy, preaching, and art of the church. Ironically, there was a renaissance of biblical studies among Jews at this period, particularly Jews living in the Islamic world; and it was at this time that the standard Massoretic text of the Hebrew Bible gradually emerged. These Jewish researches were not to have much impact on Christian biblical scholars until the end of the Middle Ages.

The invention of printing

The very first book printed from movable type is commonly agreed to have been Gutenberg's edition of the Latin Vulgate. The invention of printing coincided with the European Renaissance, and the Renaissance humanists' recovery of classical Latin and Greek, followed by some Christian study of Hebrew, inevitably led to new scholarly study of the Bible. At the same time, there was an increasing concern to diffuse Christian teachings more widely among the mass of people, and one form this concern took was vernacular translations of the Bible. It was gradually realized that printing could assist both these enterprises. Historians have often claimed that the Reformation could not have come about without printing; but the full force of this claim (as well as its complexity) has only recently become clear in Elizabeth Eisenstein's provocative *The Printing Press as an Agent of Change* (Cambridge, 2 vols., 1979), especially chapter 4, 'The Scriptural tradition recast'.

Eisenstein shows, for example, that printing on the one hand fixed the text of the Bible in a way that had never been possible before, but on the other provided the evidence to make scholars doubt whether the text could be fixed at all: there was simply too much variation and uncertainty in the tradition. When Erasmus published the first edition of the Greek New Testament in 1516, with his own Latin translation of the Greek, what immediately caught attention was how far his translation differed from the Vulgate. His Greek text is now itself considered fairly defective, but, simply because it was the first, and the science of textual criticism was undeveloped, it remained the standard text until the nineteenth century — essentially the text, for instance, that the Authorized Version is based on. Once vernacular versions such as the Authorized Version were made, and 'authorized', they gradually became the only Bible in most people's minds, so that, if any detail of them were shown to be inaccurate, the whole inspiration of the Bible seemed in doubt. Printed Bibles of course quickly made the Bible accessible to everyone who could read, but also exacerbated doctrinal disputes, because now everyone could check the texts for themselves. Not surprisingly, the Catholic Council of Trent in 1546 simply reaffirmed the authority of the Vulgate (to the astonishment of many Catholic biblical scholars), and then did its best to prevent circulation of vernacular versions.

English translations: before the Authorized Version

Unquestionably the translation of the Bible which has had the greatest impact on the English-speaking world is the Authorized Version of 1611. It ensured that the Bible, together with Shakespeare's plays, published only a few years later, was to have more influence on the subsequent development of English than any other book. Yet that version, in itself a landmark of world literature, was only the culmination of centuries of translation and controversy over translation.

Though there had been metrical paraphrases of parts of the Bible into Anglo-Saxon before 1050, the supremacy of French after the Norman Conquest, coupled with the hostility of the Western Church to vernacular scripture, ensured that, until the middle of the fourteenth century, there was little or no further attempt at translation. Between 1330 and 1350, however, two English versions of the Psalter appeared, accompanying the Latin text; one was by Richard Rolle, the hermit. Within a few years about a third of the New Testament had also been translated, though manuscripts were few, and one of the translators observed that they had been put there at some personal risk.

John Wyclif (or Wycliffe) is commonly considered to be the father of the English Bible. He was already famous as an Oxford philosopher and theologian before he founded his order of 'poor preachers', or Lollards, and instituted a programme for the translation of the entire Bible into English. How much he actually translated himself is a matter of doubt, but under his leadership the first, painfully literal, translation by the Lollards was completed about 1380. Though he was tried for heresy for questioning, among other things, the authority of the Pope and the value of monasticism, Wyclif was allowed to retire unmolested to his rectory at Lutterworth, where he died in 1384. After his death, a second revised version was completed by John Purvey in 1395. A measure of their popularity in what was still a world of laboriously copied manuscripts is that some 180 copies of the two versions survive today.

In 1408, however, the Convocation at Oxford passed a Constitution forbidding anyone, on pain of excommunication, to translate any part of the scriptures unless authorized by a bishop. Not merely was no authorization subsequently given, but the Lollards were suppressed; and to make the message even clearer, Wyclif's body at Lutterworth was dug up and thrown into the River Swift. So clear indeed was that message for more than a century that, in spite of the invention of printing in the meantime, no further attempt was made at translation. Indeed, later in the fifteenth century a Bishop of Chichester, Reginald Pecock, found himself stripped of his office and thrown into prison, just for devoting too much space in an attack on the Lollards to the dangerous subject of biblical translation.

In the early sixteenth century William Tyndale did in fact begin with an approach to the then Bishop of London, Cuthbert Tunstall, for patronage for his new translation. 'I understood at last', he concluded, 'not only that there was no room in my Lord of London's palace to translate the New Testament, but also that there was no place to do it in all England'. Moving to Wittenberg, Luther's city, he finished his translation of the New Testament in 1525. He began printing at Cologne, but by the time he had got as far as the end of St Matthew's Gospel, the town council intervened, and Tyndale fled, with the printed sheets, to Worms, where both printings were completed and dispatched to England. In pre-Reformation England it was immediately attacked by the bishops and the King, Henry VIII, as well as by the Lord Chancellor, Sir Thomas More. Copies were burned and readers persecuted. In 1531 Henry attempted to have Tyndale extradited, and, when that failed, to have him kidnapped from Antwerp. He was finally seized by the Emperor's orders in 1535, strangled, and burned at the stake at Vilvorde. By the time of his death he had published his translation of the Pentateuch (1530) and Jonah (1531), as well as two revisions of his New Testament; he had in addition made manuscript translations of Joshua to Chronicles.

A feature of English translation from Tyndale onwards is its constant and cumulative use of earlier translated material where appropriate. The so-called 'miracle' of the Authorized Version is, in fact, a palimpsest of the best of previous translations, corrected and winnowed through almost 100 years of development. Thus Coverdale's complete English Bible, printed at Cologne in 1535, is based not so much on his use of Hebrew or Greek (of which he knew little) as on Tyndale, where extant, plus Latin and German versions. Partly because Coverdale was himself a fine prose stylist, the result was remarkably successful − and though it was not licensed by the newly Protestant Henry VIII, Anne Boleyn had a copy in her chamber.

In 1537, Tyndale's disciple John Rogers, in order to preserve the still unpublished sections of the Old Testament translated by his master, produced at Antwerp, under the name of Thomas Matthew, another Bible, which incorporated all of Tyndale's work and made up what was lacking from Coverdale. This, in turn, was revised by Coverdale and became the basis of the new official, or, because of its size, so-called 'Great Bible', which Thomas Cromwell in 1537 ordered to be installed in every church for the reading of laymen. Since it was printed in Paris rather than in England or the Protestant Netherlands, it is not surprising that it fell foul of the Inquisition, who for a time confiscated the sheets, and burned a part. Coverdale escaped to England, recovered some of the missing sheets, and was able to complete the printing in England, where it was at last published in April 1539.

In 1543, however, Parliament passed a law forbidding the reading of the Bible by any but of high rank, and, with the accession of Mary ten years later, a large number of the copies of the Great Bible were again burned. Many leading Protestants went into exile, and it was one such, William Wittingham, who began in Geneva what was to be the first truly popular English translation. Among his companions in Geneva was John Knox, and to assist him in the translation there was a team that included John Bodley and his son Thomas (later to be the founder of the library at Oxford). Calvin himself wrote the introduction.

Though there had been no lack of small printed Latin Bibles, the Protestant 'open' translations, intended in theory for everyone who could read, had been in practice large and bulky — primarily designed, like the Great Bible, to be placed in churches to be read there. In contrast, the Geneva New Testament, published in 1557, was genuinely pocket-sized (duodecimo: 10 x 27.5 cm), with well-proportioned pages and, for the first time in English, divided and numbered verses — an invention of the Dominican friar Santes Pagnini and first used in a Vulgate printed at Lyon in 1527. Linked with this change in size and format was another no less significant innovation — the change from black-letter to roman type. Black-letter, based on the traditional gothic script of the hand-written Bibles, was more complicated (and therefore more expensive) to print, and, no less important, more difficult to read — especially in the new small format. Though the simpler roman type was already established in France and Italy for everything except liturgical and legal work, England, like Germany, had felt hitherto that black-letter was the appropriate form for Bible printing. Although a black-letter Geneva Bible was in fact produced in 1579, it was the 1557 Geneva version, and, later, the Authorized Version, that taught the English to prefer the simpler roman script — and made mass literacy more practicable. The pocket-sized New Testament was an instant success, and, though Elizabeth succeeded Mary as Queen in 1558, Wittingham and his colleagues stayed on in Geneva to complete (in quarto) the entire Bible, which was published in 1560.

The new Queen granted John Bodley the exclusive right for seven years, from January 1561, to print the Geneva Bible in England, but the new version soon ran into problems that were exacerbated rather than diminished by the quality of its translation and its readable format. These concerned what had become the central point of controversy in all the sixteenth-century English translations: the notes. The problems had begun with Tyndale, whose New Testament had translated the Latin *ecclesia* not by 'church' but by the more Protestant 'congregation', and whose translation of the Pentateuch had been accompanied by bitterly anti-clerical notes. His gloss on Abraham's sacrifice of Isaac, for instance, reads as follows:

Jacob robbed Laban his uncle: Moses robbed the Egyptians: And Abraham is about to slay and burn his own son: And all are holy works, because they were wrought in favour at God's command. To steal, rob and murder are no holy works before worldly people: but unto them that have their trust in God: they are holy when God commandeth them.

It is difficult to be sure of the tone of this antinomianism, but it is small wonder that the authorities were alarmed. Coverdale had continued this tradition with notes that formed in effect a strongly Protestant commentary on disputed passages, and, as might be expected from a text produced in Geneva under the patronage of Calvin himself, the new Bible had not merely marginal notes, but an introduction or 'argument' to each book of the Bible, giving where appropriate a strongly Calvinist interpretation. Such interpretations were not merely a theological matter − they also pointed politically towards republicanism. The Elizabethan Anglican settlement had been a delicate theological and political compromise − the 1559 Act of Uniformity had been passed by only three votes in the House of Commons, and in the Lords not a single Bishop had voted for it. While it was politically impossible to ban the new Bible, its overt Calvinist bias made it a centre of potential controversy and danger.

To meet this problem, the bishops, under the new Archbishop of Canterbury, Matthew Parker, produced the 'Bishops' Bible' in 1568, the year of the expiry of Bodley's patent. It was a sumptuously printed folio in black-letter text with marginal notes − and conspicuously failed either to sell substantially or to satisfy its critics. While the format ensured that it did not compete in popularity with the Geneva Bible, its notes placated neither Calvinists nor their opponents. It did not achieve the imprimatur of the Convocation of Canterbury until 1571, and in the end it never received the authority of the Privy Council at all. By contrast, in 1575–6 London editions of the Geneva New Testament and full Bible were finally produced, with further printings in Scotland (1576 and 1579 respectively). Before it was finally superseded in England by the Authorized Version in 1611, the Geneva Bible had gone through nearly 150 separate editions, and had established its format as standard for the English family Bible.

The Authorized Version

The accession of James I to the combined throne of England and Scotland was the signal for renewed pressure for puritan reforms in the liturgy and discipline of the Church of England. At a conference of divines convened by the King at Hampton Court in 1603, the Bishop of London, Richard Bancroft, was at first against any new translation: 'if every man's humour might be followed, there would be no end of translating . . .' James, however, was in favour: 'I profess I could never yet see a Bible well translated in English; but I think that of all, that of Geneva is the worst. I wish some special pains were taken for an uniform translation; which should be done by the best learned in both universities, then reviewed by the bishops, presented to the privy council, lastly ratified by royal authority to be read in the whole church and no other'. 'But it is fit that no marginal notes be added thereunto', rejoined Bancroft. The King could not but agree: 'That caveat is well put in; for in the Genevan translation some notes are partial, untrue, seditious, and savouring of traitorous conceits . . .'

The ground rules for the new translation laid down as a result of this debate indicate very clearly what was to be expected of the projected Authorized Version (AV). It was from the start deliberately conceived as a document of political and theological compromise. Among the instructions given were:

i. The ordinary Bible read in the church, commonly called the Bishop's Bible, to be followed, and as little altered as the original will permit.

ii. The names of the prophets and the holy writers, with other names in the text, to be retained as near as may be, accordingly as they are vulgarly used.

iii. The old ecclesiastical words to be kept, viz. as the word *church* not to be translated *congregation* &c.

iv. When any word hath divers significations, that to be kept which hath been most commonly used by the most eminent fathers, being agreeable to the propriety of the place and the analogy of faith.

v. The division of chapters to be altered either not at all, or as little as may be, if necessity so require.

vi. No marginal notes at all to be affixed, but only for the explanation of the Hebrew and Greek words which cannot without some circumlocution so briefly and fitly be expressed in the text. . .

xiv. These translations to be used when they agree better with the text than the Bishop's Bible, viz. Tindal's, Matthew's, Coverdale's, Whitchurch, Geneva.

Not merely was it intended that, where it was useful or politically expedient, this version should be heavily reliant on the collective endeavours of earlier translations, but this element of collectivity and consensus was heavily reinforced by an elaborate committee structure, which ensured that each of the forty-seven appointed translators had his individual work reviewed by the others in his group, and the work of each group was then reviewed by all the other groups. Finally, two members from each of the three centres of translation, Cambridge, Oxford, and Westminster, were chosen to review the entire Bible and to prepare the work for publication in London. There was to be no individual idiosyncrasy authorized in this version. It is frequently said that committees encourage mediocrity and are inimical to the production of great art or literature; but if a camel is a horse designed by a committee, then the AV is the ultimate camel.

This explicit commitment both to tradition and consensus left its mark on the text in two very important ways. Firstly, it meant that the language of the translation was deliberately archaic. In a period when the English language was changing more rapidly than ever before or since, the Bible was set in words that were designed to stress the essential continuity of the Anglican settlement with the past by recalling the phraseology, not merely of the familiar Geneva Bible, but of Coverdale and Tyndale — and beyond that even of the Vulgate itself. At a time of threatened disorder — that within a generation was to culminate in Civil War — the new Bible was a statement of stability, order, and above all continuity with the past. It was, in the fullest sense of the word, a political document.

Secondly, there was no room for individual interpretation. Not merely was it politically inexpedient; it was also theologically inappropriate and even, in extreme cases, blasphemous. If the Bible was inspired by the Holy Spirit and was the source of its own authority, then it was doubly dangerous for man to seek to amend it in any way. Indeed Nicholas von Wyle, a fifteenth-century German translator, had gone so far as to declare that, in the case of the Bible, even copyists' errors should be faithfully transcribed. The King James translators had the added sanction of the Catholic translators of the Rheims and Douai Bibles — the Old Testament, by the latter group, had only just appeared in 1609, after a delay of twenty-seven years — who had attacked their Protestant rivals for softening the hard places, whereas they themselves, they claimed, 'religiously keep them word for word, and point for point, for fear of missing or restraining the sense of the holy Ghost to our phantasie . . .'. Thus John Boyes (or Bois), a fellow of St John's College, Cambridge, who was both a translator of a section of the New Testament for the AV and a member of the final revision panel, recorded in his notes that he and his committee had been careful to preserve ambiguities in the original text. Referring to the word 'praise' in I Peter 1:7, which might refer either to Jesus or to the members of the Church, he commented that 'We have not thought that the indefinite ought to be defined'. Seventeenth-century translators, whether Protestant or Catholic, were under no doubt that, whatever the difficulties or peculiarities of the Hebrew or Greek, they were there for a divinely ordained purpose, and were therefore not to be corrected by human agency.

Yet this manifest unwillingness to limit the meaning of the

inspired words of scripture by translation did not hamper the translators linguistically as much as a modern reader might expect. Their deliberate choice of matching ambiguity with ambiguity was aided by both the range of meanings available to seventeenth-century English and − just as important − the translators' sensitivity to that range. For example, in Tyndale's translation John 8:46 is rendered 'Which of you can rebuke me of sin?' Instead of following this perfectly intelligible reading, the AV has chosen the much more obscure 'Which of you convinceth me of sin?' The Greek word in question is *elencho*, which is translated at different points in the AV by no less than six English words: 'convince, 'convict', 'tell one's fault', 'reprove', 'discover', and (as Tyndale had it here) 'rebuke'. Why then the need to depart from Tyndale's reading at this point? The answer seems to lie with the history of that word 'convince'. Though the *OED* allows only one current meaning of the word, it also lists seven other obsolete senses − all of which were current in the early seventeenth century. Lady Macbeth, for instance, says of Duncan's chamberlains:

> Will I with wine and wassail so convince
> That memory, the warder of the brain,
> Shall be a fume, and the receipt of reason
> A limbeck only? (1, vii, 64–7)

Most Shakespeare glossaries suggest that 'convince' here means 'overpower', but other meanings of the word, such as 'to prove a person guilty . . . especially by judicial procedure' or 'to disprove, refute' or 'to demonstrate or prove absurdity', all suggest how Lady Macbeth's mind is racing ahead to visualize how the grooms might be overpowered, their protestations swept aside and refuted as absurd, and finally convicted. Similarly, in the AV's careful substitution of 'convince' for 'rebuke', we can catch a hint that Jesus is challenging the whole network of semi-judicial accusations flung against him as absurd − without, of course, allowing the reader to lose sight of the fact that one day soon these will indeed overpower him, and bring him to the ultimate absurdity of the cross.

Something of the care with which these particular words were chosen is indicated by a later passage in John 16:8: 'And when he is come, he will reprove the world of sin, and of righteousness, and of judgement.' Though the selected translation of *elencho* here is 'reprove' (again replacing 'rebuke' in Tyndale), the translators have also added 'convince' in the margin. Whether or not this indicates some shade of disagreement among them, it serves to emphasize how closely the words 'reprove' and 'convince' were associated in their minds. It is such sensitivities both to the nuances of individual words, and to their relationship to the larger rhythms of the Bible, that makes the AV so remarkable a translation.

Modern translations

This attitude towards language followed directly from the theological principles of the AV translators; for the same reason, it could not survive the critical revolution of the eighteenth century. The principles of higher criticism had immediate consequences for what is less often called 'lower criticism' — the detail of textual scholarship itself. Because, for instance, a growing knowledge of the historical context revealed that for the Hebrews the liver was the seat of the emotions, the slight change necessary to render 'my heart is glad and my glory rejoiceth' (Psalm 16:9), to '. . . my liver rejoiceth', seemed more accurate, if, to the modern ear, less elevated. Other equally likely cases of straight mis-translation threatened to have much more serious theological consequences, however. No textual change in the Hebrew is necessary at all to substitute the more accurate 'young woman' for the Septuagint's 'virgin' in the famous passage from Isaiah 7:14: 'behold! a virgin shall conceive and bear a son', but the doctrinal implications were enough to make the reading highly controversial.

A growing knowledge of such anomalies, as well as of the biblical world, had stimulated a series of translations of individual books of the Bible from the later seventeenth century onwards. Yet it would be a mistake to see too sharp a division between the ways in which typological and historical theories of interpretation affected translation theory. Lowth himself had followed up his *Lectures on the Sacred Poetry of the Hebrews* with a new translation of Isaiah in 1778. In the Preface he explains his own principles:

The first and principal business of a Translator is to give us the plain literal and grammatical sense of the author; the obvious meaning of his words, phrases, and sentences, and to express them in the language into which he translates, as far as may be, in equivalent words, phrases, and sentences . . . This is peculiarly so in subjects of high importance such as the Holy Scriptures, in which so much depends on the phrase and expression; and particularly in the Prophetical books of scripture; where from the letter are often deduced deep and recondite senses, which must owe all their weight and solidity to the just and accurate interpretation of the words of the Prophecy. For whatever senses are supposed to be included in the Prophet's words, Spiritual, Mystical, Allegorical, Anagogical, or the like, they must all entirely depend on the literal sense.
(*Isaiah: A New Translation* (1778), Edinburgh, 5th edn, 1807, Vol. 1, p. lxx)

With hindsight, such an argument can justly be seen as transitional, in that it justifies modern textual procedures by claiming that they provide a more scholarly basis for traditional modes of exegesis; but we must remember that it would not have appeared to Lowth in this way. For him, as for many of his contemporaries, there was no evident incompatibility between the historical methods of higher criticism, and mystical and typological hermeneutics. He is under no doubt, for instance, that the ultimate meaning of Isaiah's prophecies is to herald the coming of Jesus: 'This seems to me to be the nature and true design of this part of Isaiah's prophecies; and this view of them seems to afford the best method of resolving difficulties, in which the Expositors are frequently engaged, being much divided between what is called the Literal and Mystical sense, properly; for the mystical or spiritual sense is very often the most literal sense of all'.

The Revised Version

No new version of the entire Bible, however, was attempted until that of the Revised Version (RV), completed in 1885. In keeping with the conservatism traditional to the English in such matters, the brief to the revisers was cautious in the extreme. They were not to alter the existing language of the AV except where absolutely necessary for the sense, and the composition of the panels themselves (as it was sarcastically observed, with a high proportion of schoolmasters) ensured that these instructions were themselves interpreted with extreme conservatism. Neither of the examples given on p. 123 was, in fact, altered, and some of the alterations made were only marginally clearer. Ezekiel 27:25, for instance, which the AV had given as 'the ships of Tarshish did sing of them in thy market', became scarcely less enigmatically 'were caravans for thy merchandise'. What the revisers did do with stubborn pedantry in the New Testament was to try and render the same Greek word by the same English word throughout – a practice which the seventeenth-century translators had explicitly avoided – and treated New Testament Greek as though it were that of the classical period. Thus 'we have toiled all night and took nothing' (Luke 5:5) was changed to 'we toiled all night and took nothing', simply in order to try and reproduce an aorist tense in English. It seems that even if the AV had miraculously managed to evade the fate normally reserved for works generated by committee, the RV was a reassertion of the general truth of the rule. Though it did represent a genuine improvement in scholarship over its predecessor, it was, not surprisingly, never popular with the public, and in literary terms it made almost no impact at all.

The New English Bible and the Good News Bible

The wave of more radical new translations that followed the Second World War was supported by the much wider publicity available to modern marketing, and sales of the principal translations have run into millions. Yet they have not been without their critics – not least those who, without any particular religious interest in the text, regretted the wholesale sweeping away of hallowed phraseology, on straightforwardly literary grounds. Kenneth Grayston, one of the translators of the New English Bible (NEB) (1961), has acknowledged the force of some of these criticisms:

The New English Bible does not compete with the Authorised Version, certainly not in language and style: this is not a period of great writers equal to Spenser, Sidney, Hooker, Marlowe and Shakespeare. Modern English, it seems to me, is slack instead of taut, verbose and not concise, infested with this month's cliché, no longer the language of a proud and energetic English people, but an international means of communication. And 'means of communication' gives the game away: it seems to me a repository for the bad habits of foreigners speaking English. This is how we must speak if people are to listen and grasp what we say.
('Confessions of a biblical translator', *New Universities Quarterly*, Summer 1979, p. 287)

Such pessimism about the state of twentieth–century English (not to mention the gratuitous hint of xenophobia) is fortunately not shared by all modern critics − though it is worth noticing that Milton bewailed the degenerate state of his language, its fads and its susceptibility to foreign influence, only a generation after the publication of the AV. But one consequence of such debates is that, because they have focused on obvious and sometimes superficial changes in phraseology − 'you' for 'thee' and 'thou', for instance − they have distracted attention from much more sweeping changes, both in the state of the English language itself and in the actual theory of translation that underlies the new versions.

Though it is debatable whether English has been damaged (as Grayston claims), or enriched, by becoming a world language, it is unquestionably true that it has changed in significant ways since the seventeenth century. Changes in language, moreover, reveal changing patterns of thought. There is a good example of such a change in I Corinthians 15:33, where Paul quotes the Greek classical author, Menander: 'evil communications corrupt good manners'. The word here translated as 'manners' by both Tyndale and the AV is the Greek word *ethos*, in the plural *ethe*. It is defined as 'an accustomed place, custom, usage, the manners and habits of man, his disposition and character, especially moral character' (Liddell & Scott). As Paul was well aware, Menander was using *ethe* in its full secular sense to cover all the above meanings. In English also, 'manner' can mean 'custom' − and the *OED* indicates that, in the seventeenth century, the plural signified 'a person's habitual behaviour, or conduct; moral character or morals'. In the nineteenth century John Keble, one of the leaders of the Oxford Movement, made a deliberate attempt to revive this integration of behaviour and morals by coining a new English word directly from the Greek: 'ethos'. It was above all intended to describe a quality of Oxford life that left a lasting mark upon its graduates: a quality closely associated with that other Victorian concept, the 'gentleman' − described once by Coleridge's nephew, J. T. Coleridge, as implying no 'intellectual quality, scarcely even any distinct moral one, but an habitual toning, or colouring diffused over all a man's qualities, giving the exercise of them a peculiar gentleness and grace' (*Memoir of The Rev. John Keble* (1869), pp. 384–5). The problem for modern translators is that in contemporary English that once self-evident connection has been lost − and Keble's attempt to bring it within a particular educational and social context has probably made it impossible to revive the Greek root in the Pauline sense. As a result, we find that none of the recent translations can take on board more than one third of what *ethe* (or the seventeenth-century 'manners') stood for. Thus the RV, the Revised Standard Version, and the New American Bible have here 'morals'; J. B. Phillips has 'conduct'; and the NEB, the Good News Bible (GNB), and the New International Version have 'character'. Though here it is no fault of the translators, each version is fragmentary and partial, and all have lost that sense of the subtle interaction of morals and custom as a source for behaviour that could only exist in a more integrated and less pluralistic society than our own.

Changes in the theory of translation have been no less sweeping over the same period. If the keynote of the RV was pedantic caution, no one could accuse the translators of the NEB of the same fault. Grayston has described the aims of his team as follows: 'We have conceived our task to be that of understanding the original as precisely as we could (using all available aids) and then saying again in our native idiom what we believed the author to be saying in his . . . And so, in equivocal passages, the translators had to come off the fence and say, "we think it means this". In ambiguous passages they had to write out the meaning plainly, and in obscure passages, to refrain from reproducing nonsense in translation' (*Confessions*, p. 288). Nor was the panel responsible for the NEB unusual in its desire to break with the attempts of past translators to recapture the ambiguities of the original texts. By and large, twentieth-century translation has commonly held to the principle that a clear reading in English, even if it involves paraphrase, is better than accuracy to a doubtful original.

Those responsible for the Good News Bible (1976) were, if possible, even more forthright than the translators of the NEB in their intentions. According to the preface, 'The primary concern of the translators has been to provide a faithful translation of the meaning of the Hebrew, Aramaic and Greek texts. Their first task was to understand correctly the meaning of the original . . . The translators' next task was to express that meaning in a manner and form easily understood by the readers . . . Every effort has been made to use language that is natural, clear, simple and unambiguous'. For Eugene A. Nida, one of the leading figures in the American Bible Society, which was responsible for the GNB, 'Translating consists in producing in the receptor language the closest natural equivalent to the message of the source language, first in meaning and secondly in style . . . By "natural" we mean that the equivalent forms should not be "foreign" either in form . . . or meaning. That is to say, a good translation should not reveal its non-native source' ('In praise of metaphrase', in vol. 6 of *Comparative Criticism*, ed. E. S. Shaffer, Cambridge, 1984).

In contrast to the attitude of the earlier translators, the assumption here is that the problem lies not in the 'message' of the text, but in its translation into an 'equivalent form' in English. For Nida there are basically two kinds of equivalence, which he calls 'formal' and 'dynamic'. In his words, formal equivalence 'focuses attention on the message itself, in both form and content. In such translation one is concerned with such correspondences as poetry to poetry, sentence to sentence, and concept to concept'. The aim is the traditional one of keeping as faithfully to the original as possible. Dynamic equivalence, on the other hand, is what we see at work in the GNB. Its purpose is not so much to stay close to the sense of the original as to create an equivalent *effect* to that existing in the source language. This, according to Nida, is what a biblical translator should be attempting. One of his most telling examples is that of a particular African tribe where beating one's chest is a sign of pride, and clubbing one's head a sign of humility and repentence. For such a culture, the story of the Pharisee and the publican (Luke 18:10–14), where the publican 'smote his breast, saying, God be merciful to me a sinner', is clearly meaningless until it is translated into appropriate *cultural* terms. Whatever it says in the Greek, for that African language at least the unfortunate sinner must club his head.

Certainly such an approach does remove and clarify many of the more blatant corruptions in the Hebrew and Greek texts. The enigmatic reference to the 'ships of Tarshish' which 'did sing of thee in thy market' (Ezekiel 27:25) is rendered more reasonably by the GNB as 'Your merchandise was carried in fleets of the largest cargo ships' — though the idea of a fleet of cargo ships singing praise to its owner or nation, simply by the wealth and splendour of its merchandise, is a conceit that would not have seemed too far-fetched to the contemporaries of John Donne. Other probable corruptions which the more cautious translators of the RV had also left intact are clarified. For instance, Psalm 11:6, in the AV reads 'upon the wicked He shall rain snares, fire and brimstone and an horrible tempest'. 'Snares' (or 'traps') is again an unlikely reading, and in fact only the most minute alteration of the Hebrew pointing is required to change 'snares' to the more probable 'coals'. The GNB reads: 'He sends down flaming coals and burning sulphur on the wicked; he punishes them with scorching winds', adding a footnote to explain how it has amended the Hebrew 'traps'. This is unexceptionable textually, but in addition to altering 'traps' to 'coals' the GNB has introduced its own (quite unauthenticated) 'Hebrew parallelism': setting the 'scorching winds' over against the 'flaming coals and burning sulphur' rather than being the third term in the triad. The effect is to suggest, not one kind of cataclysmic event (a reference presumably to the fate of the 'cities of the plain', Sodom and Gomorrah, in Genesis 20), but *two* quite separate ones: if not fire and brimstone (on their cities?), then scorching winds (on their crops?). It is difficult to know if this is an example of substituting an equivalent cultural effect − atomic holocausts, perhaps, and dustbowls in the Midwest − or merely the kind of lack of attention to exact wording that we have already noted as characteristic of modern translation theory.

Nida's whole case, of course, rests on the unargued pre-supposition that all the necessary equivalent cultural effects *do* actually exist in the receptor language. Yet there is considerable evidence to suggest that, historically, it has been precisely in those cases where there was no appropriate equivalent that the greatest impact on the receptor language has resulted. Thus, for instance, the very first major biblical translation, the Septuagint, revealed its 'non-native source' in a way that was to have a profound effect on the subsequent development of Greek. Because the Hebrew word *kabod* (whose original root meant 'weight' but which had at some stage since the time of Ezekiel come to mean also 'glory') was translated by the Greek word *doxa* (which had originally meant something nearer 'appearance' or 'reputation'), the latter word quickly gained the additional connotations of 'radiance' and 'splendour' in other non-religious Greek contexts. Similarly the translation of the Bible into English in the sixteenth century had the incidental effect of modifying the English language. There is a story (possibly apocryphal) that when the translators of the NEB came to the parable of the Prodigal Son they decided to find out the modern English equivalent of the 'fat-ted calf'. Accordingly, they consulted a butcher at Smithfield market in London as to what one called a calf that had been specially fattened up for a particular occasion. He explained that the technical phrase was 'fatted calf' − and that it came from the Bible! More generally, perhaps, too little attention has been paid to the way in which Western Europe, with its cool temperate climate and abundant rainfall, was able to assimilate and make use of the everyday imagery of a semi-nomadic Near Eastern desert people as part of its own cultural and poetic heritage. For 'shame cultures' whose morality is traditionally based upon external public observances, the evolving Hebrew sense of sin and the New Testament stress on internal self-regulation is bound to be deeply alien — and without equivalencies. Indeed, it has been argued, *contra* Nida, that a language develops in range and subtlety of expression not through its receptivity to translation, but through its *resistance* to new words and concepts. 'In translating', wrote Goethe, 'we must go to the brink of the Untranslatable; it is only then that we really become aware of the foreignness of the nation and the language.'

This leads us directly back to the hermeneutical problem that has always been inseparable from the history of the Bible. What about those instances where a strangeness in the original text signals an essential strangeness in meaning? where there is *no* equivalence, because what is being described is something genuinely new in human experience? In I Kings 19:12, for instance, the literal English translation of the Hebrew *kol demamah dakkah* is 'a small (or thin) voice of silence'. The AV, with its scrupulous care for what it held to be the language of the Holy Spirit, translates this curious oxymoron by the well-known 'still small voice', thus keeping the sense of paradox or peculiarity that is surely the essence of the original. Modern translations, however, presumably with the principle of dynamic equivalence in mind, have unanimously chosen to remove this paradox in favour of naturalistic paraphrase. Thus the NEB offers us 'a low murmuring sound'; the GNB 'the soft whisper of a voice'; and the Catholic Jerusalem Bible 'the sound of a gentle breeze'. None has even attempted to capture the ambiguity between divine and natural agency so important to the original, or, consequently, to contrast it with the natural violence of the earthquake, wind and fire that preceded it. The possibility that this disjunction is itself important to the whole action of the story is not apparently considered. There seems to be no place in these translations for that encounter with the 'other', the numinous, that has historically been an essential component of religious experience. What is disturbing in such instances is not the modern language, but the assumption, so clearly expressed in the preface to the GNB, that the Bible (and by inference, religious experience) can be reduced to things that are 'natural, clear, simple and unambiguous' — a conclusion that would have greatly puzzled the sixteenth- and seventeenth-century translators, not to mention a long procession of saints, mystics, and poets over the last 2000 years.

The Bible and English literature

As we saw in the first chapter, there is a sense in which the Bible has given a particular shape to the whole development of European literature, providing a model of unity with diversity, and creating an expectation of inner meaning and moral development within the narrative frame. The literature about the Bible itself is so vast that we can hardly begin to list it. Milton's *Paradise Lost, Paradise Regained,* and *Samson Agonistes*, for instance, all depend directly on the reader's previous knowledge of the relevant scriptural passages. In modern times the Bible has provided plots for Thomas Mann's *Joseph and his Brothers*, several plays of James Bridie, and innumerable Hollywood epics, culminating, in expense at least, with Cecil B. de Mille's *The Ten Commandments*. In a slightly less direct but no less profound way it has inspired Dante's *Divine Comedy*, Langland's *Piers Ploughman*, Bunyan's *Pilgrim's Progress*, and the prophetic books of Blake. Indeed the literature of Europe is steeped in biblical reference and allusion at every level. Not least because of the peculiar history and strengths of the AV, this influence has nowhere been more marked or pervasive than in the development of English literature.

Thus, even before we turn to the influence of specific biblical themes on English literature, we find that the whole idea of literature, its interpretation, its evaluation, and even its diction and metaphorical structure, is shot through with assumptions and patterns of thought taken from the Bible. Such underlying patterns help to explain the way in which the major biblical themes fell in England on ground so fertile that the whole development of its literature can sometimes seem like little more than an extended commentary on the one Book. Even that proverbial metaphor, of seed falling on fertile ground, is itself biblical in origin — taken from the parable of the Sower (Matthew 13:3–8). Yet the transmutation of biblical themes into secular literature is not just a process of either re-telling or of commentary. It starts, as we have seen, with the idea of a book itself. We find hints of it as early as Chaucer, but it is significant that the rise of the novel, with its stress less on the outward actions of characters than on their inward desires and feelings, should coincide with the eighteenth-century rediscovery of the Bible as a model of literary taste. Thus Mrs Trimmer in 1806 introduces her apparently very conventional commentary on the Bible in terms that would have been unthinkable before the rise of the novel:

The Histories . . . differ from all other histories that were ever written, for they give an account of the *ways of God*; and explain *why GOD protected and rewarded* some persons and nations, and *why* he *punished* others; also *what led* particular persons mentioned in Scripture to *do* certain things for which they were approved or condemned; whereas writers who compose histories in a common way, without being inspired of GOD, can only form guesses and conjectures concerning God's dealings with mankind, neither can they know what passed in the hearts of those they write about; such knowledge as this, belongs to GOD alone, whose ways are *unsearchable and past finding out, and to whom all hearts are open, all desires known!* (p. iii)

The God-like omnipotence of the novelist had already been taken up by Fielding in *Tom Jones*. In the course of a whole series of comparisons of himself, as author, with a cook, a judge, a dramatist, and a governor, Fielding explicitly compares himself with the Author of the book of nature: like the Almighty, the novelist creates his own universe with its peculiar inhabitants, laws, and events. The reader is thus warned 'not too hastily to condemn any of the Incidents in this our history, as impertinent and foreign to our main design, because thou dost not immediately conceive in what manner such incident may conduce to that design. This work may, indeed, be considered as a great creation of our own . . .' (1966 edn, p. 467). The novelist here is less an exegete than a Calvinistic God. Because the reader, like fallen man, cannot appreciate the whole mysterious outworkings of the plot, he cannot judge it. At one level, of course, this is theological parody, but there is also a serious point about textual interpretation here, one that a medieval writer such as Dante would have understood and appreciated.

With hindsight it is easy to observe how this process of 'internalization' that was to become such a marked feature of Romantic and post-Romantic literature had long been a characteristic − if unexpectedly awkward − feature of literary adaptations of biblical themes. Take, for instance, the story of the Fall. We have no reason to believe that Milton, in writing *Paradise Lost*, did not believe in the absolute literal truth of the story he was relating. But, as we have seen, that literal truth signified for him something different from what it would have for, say, a nineteenth-century fundamentalist, if only because the literal was just one, and possibly the least important one, of many levels of meaning encoded in the narrative. Nevertheless, there was no possibility of tampering with the basic events in the way that Shakespeare was able to do with Holinshed. This, after all, was Holy Writ. Yet, as a succession of critics from Blake onwards have pointed out, something rather strange has happened to the fundamental nature of the story as it appears in that monumental poem. The original biblical narrative is spare and stark in the extreme. It is told in a third-person voice which is not that of God, or of Man, or of Satan. In other words, it is already transmitted in a literary − or, to be more exact, mythical − form. In contrast, Milton's narrative is polyphonous. God, Adam and Eve, and, most important of all, Satan have all acquired distinctive voices, with characters and motives to match. In consequence, not merely has the Fall been dramatized in a way quite foreign to the original Genesis story, but in the process it has also been inescapably internalized. No longer can the stress be laid upon the act of eating the forbidden fruit; we must take into account the motives for that action. Satan's is patently revenge − not a motive even hinted at in the Bible narrative. Eve's are more complicated. She desires the divine status that she seems to be offered, but not just for its own sake: she wants to share it with Adam − partly, it is true, to impress him, but partly too out of desire to *give* something to the man who, literally, has everything. Adam's are less complex, but in their own way even less reprehensible. He loves Eve. He weighs the consequences carefully. He even goes so far as to consider that, if he rejects her now, God might simply blot her out and give him a new and better model woman. That decides him. He will stand by her, come what may. But by this time something catastrophic has happened to the original myth of the Fall. So far from being deliberate disobedience, it has turned into something suspiciously like an exercise in love and loyalty.

Nor is this all. The moment we start to consider motive rather than just deed, it is clear that, in order to contemplate disobeying God, the Fall must already have taken place. If Eve simply contemplates trying to alter her status in the order of creation, she is *already* guilty of pride; Adam, weighing his loyalty to God against his loyalty to Eve, though he may well be technically guilty of the same sin, is already moving into the much more complex world of moral choice between different, incompatible values − a dilemma that anyone who had lived in mid seventeenth-century England and the Civil War would have known with peculiar poignancy. Either way, the original myth has been inescapably changed in a manner that we must presume could not have been consciously anticipated by either Milton or his seventeenth-century audience.

Yet we must be wary of taking this as evidence that the literary process of internalization that we have noted above in some way invalidates the myth itself. On the contrary, the internalizing or psychologizing of the myth was actually to give it new and unpredictable resonances. William Golding, for instance, writing 300 years after Milton, in the mid twentieth century, sees that process of internalizing that we associate with the later development of literature as a crucial aspect of the Fall itself. In his novel *The Inheritors* (1955) he portrays a species of un-fallen Neanderthals who have no sense of themselves as differentiated from their natural environment. Though they can use a few simple words, they prefer to communicate telepathically by means of direct pictures in the mind. The essential feature of this mode of communication, of course, is that there is no possibility of concealment. There is, as it were, no space, no privacy for self-consciousness in our sense – and therefore no room for either lies or deceit. Such a space, Golding suggests, is the creation of language. The technology of violence is premeditated and therefore linguistic, and with language goes loss of innocence. Thus a bow is not something menacing that requires evasive action; it is simply seen as a stick that shortens at both ends. The few words the Neanderthals possess are studiedly empty of cause, effect, and time. Things just are. Unfortunately, such pictures and their appropriate vocabulary are not equipped to encounter change. The novel is set at the end of the Ice Age; the landscape is thawing and great lakes and rivers are appearing; on the water come the new people armed with bows and arrows – and one doesn't use poisoned arrows for food one is intending to eat. Neanderthal man has encountered *homo sapiens*, and is on his way to extinction. Post-lapsarian articulate and technological humanity has arrived.

So, of course, has the novel. Language has not only created space between thought and action, it has also enabled us to distinguish between them, and to be aware that we do so. As we have suggested, the true test of consciousness is in the ability to lie – or, as here, to create fictions. Certainly for Golding the origins of narrative are rooted in the very myth of the Fall itself – and it is no accident that, at the centre of the spiritual geography of *The Inheritors* is a huge frozen ice-age waterfall that blocks the path of both Neanderthals and *homo sapiens* on their journey inland to escape the rising waters. In the end it is the innocent but unreflecting Neanderthals who are defeated by it, for they fear water; as the ice melts, breaks up and turns into a raging torrent, it is the humans who successfully scale the fall and launch themselves onto the hitherto uncharted waters of the inland sea. The symbolism is obvious enough; perhaps less obvious, but in the light of his later work equally important, is the fact that the fable relates not merely to the origins of evil, but also, reflexively, to the origins of the artist's own medium of words — and not least, of course, to the words of the scriptures.

If we think of the commentary on Genesis and the Gospel of John (even perhaps Revelation) implied here, even the title *The Inheritors* takes on a new resonance. We, the human race, are the inheritors not just of the earth but of a tradition. The point, once again, is simply that the idea of a book is not something that comes to us innocent or empty-handed. On the contrary, it has been culturally conditioned by the historical presence of the Bible, and its relationship to subsequent thought, in very particular and highly complex ways. So central were these to our own culture that for long periods it was only by a very self-conscious effort that it was possible to focus on them at all. As long as narrative could be seen simply as a literary concomitant of the notion of historical progress, the fact that it was born of a need to reinterpret a problematic and threatening past could conveniently be forgotten. With the ending of the Second World War, and the revelations of the full extent of Nazi atrocities (not to mention Allied responses), the question of human nature and history became a problem of a kind not seen, in England at any rate, since the end of the Civil War. Those revelations meant that nineteenth-century meliorist interpretations of history, and liberal assumptions of progress, were open to question in a quite new way. Prominent among those ideas had been the easy optimism of socio-biological developmental theories promulgated by such works as H. G. Wells' *Outline of History* (1920), which Golding actually quotes as a preface to his fable. Golding's stark and disturbing story, however, holds the mirror up to a very different world from that of Wells' late nineteenth-century England. For Golding, the entire text of human history had to be re-read and re-interpreted in the light of its most recent ending. But such a re-reading is never a one-way process: in so far as that re-reading modified our idea of humanity, it also modified our idea of language and of books.

Yet that point raises a further one. What we have here, of course, is more than just a reinterpretation and internalization of the biblical myth of the Fall, linking the origins of evil, as well as good, with the creation of the Word. In the light of the process of commentary and revision that has always been central to the making of the Bible, it is possible to see such works as *Paradise Lost* and *The Inheritors* as direct continuations of a process of debate now at least 3000 years old. It so happens that the biblical canon has been finally established and closed for just under two of those millennia. There is no chance now that *Paradise Lost* could be included in it — but once we start to see the Bible not in terms of a static and therefore time-bound revelation, but as the continuous and ongoing self-referential debate over the nature of man and God, good and evil, words and the Word, that it has always been, there is nothing intrinsically absurd about the idea. The reasons for exclusion of Milton or Golding are entirely contingent, rather than necessary. The gap separating the two writers is less than half that separating the oldest and newest books of the Bible. If the mode of hermeneutical interpretation has changed between Milton and Golding, there are changes as great, stemming from experience as bitter, within the books of the established biblical canon. The referential strength of the underlying biblical myth, and its sense of polysemous meaning, is as creative as ever. In the course of this brief work we have tried to show that the Bible, the 'book of books', is not merely the most profound single cultural and religious influence on our civilization, but the paradigm of a debate and a questioning that is central to our unfolding knowledge of what it is to be fully human.

Guide to further reading

Translations of the Bible

The Authorized, or King James, Version is available in innumerable editions. Readers may find the editions called 'The Bible Designed to be Read as Literature' useful, in that they print the poetic passages in verse form; on the other hand, they do not give verse numbers. The Revised Standard Version also exists in many editions; that by Herbert G. May and Bruce M. Metzger (*The New Oxford Annotated Bible with the Apocrypha: Revised Standard Version*, New York, revised edn, 1977) includes textual notes, short introductions, general annotations, and cross references. The New English Bible has just been revised as *The Revised English Bible with the Apocrypha* (Oxford and Cambridge, 1989); it includes some section headings, and textual notes, but no cross references. The Jerusalem Bible has been revised as *The New Jerusalem Bible* (London and New York, 1985). It includes fairly detailed introductions and notes, which give attention to questions of literary form; its Catholic theological position is fairly unobtrusive; it uses 'Yahweh' rather than 'the Lord' throughout the Old Testament; and it is particularly useful for tracing 'themes' through the Bible. The most recent translation of the Hebrew Bible by Jewish scholars is *Tanakh: a New Translation of the Holy Scriptures according to the Traditional Hebrew Text* (Philadelphia, 1985). Concordances to the Bible are helpful for tracing quotations and themes. There is a famous 'Biblical Concordance' to the Authorized Version by Alexander Cruden, which has appeared since 1737 in many forms. Of more recent works the following is particularly useful: Richard E. Whitaker, *The Eerdmans Analytical Concordance to the Revised Standard Version* (Grand Rapids, Michigan, 1988). For study of the New Testament Gospels a 'synopsis' is recommended, particularly: Kurt Aland, *Synopsis of the Four Gospels*, English Edition, Completely Revised (New York, 1982).

Bible dictionaries

The following are especially recommended: Paul J. Achtemeier, ed., *Harper's Bible Dictionary* (San Francisco, 1985), which gives concise

139

and up-to-date information on every character, place, book, literary form, and theme in the Bible; and *The Interpreters' Dictionary of the Bible* (Nashville, Tennessee, 4 vols., 1962, with *Supplementary Volume*, 1976), which does the same at greater length.

Bible commentaries

The following one-volume commentaries on the whole Bible are particularly recommended: James L. Mays, ed., *Harper's Bible Commentary* (San Francisco, 1988) and Raymond E. Brown and others, eds., *The New Jerome Biblical Commentary* (New York, 1989).

Introductions to the Bible and to the Hebrew Bible and the New Testament

Robert Alter and Frank Kermode, eds., *The Literary Guide to the Bible* (Cambridge, Mass., 1987) has been widely hailed as a watershed in literary reading of the Bible. It was planned in conscious opposition to many 'critical introductions' to the Bible. Of the latter the following are among the most recent: Rolf Rendtorff, *The Old Testament: an Introduction* (London, 1985); Luke T. Johnson, *The Writings of the New Testament: an Interpretation* (Philadelphia, 1986); and Helmut Koester, *Introduction to the New Testament* (Berlin, 2 vols., 1982). (The Koester is in many ways the climactic work of the 'Bultmann tradition' in twentieth-century New Testament scholarship).

Histories of scholarship

The following are particularly up-to-date and thorough: Douglas A. Knight and Gene M. Tucker, eds., *The Hebrew Bible and its Modern Interpreters* (Atlanta, Georgia, 1985); Robert A. Kraft and George W. E. Nickelsburg, eds., *Early Judaism and its Modern Interpreters* (Atlanta, 1986); and Eldon J. Epp and George W. Macrae, eds., *The New Testament and its Modern Interpreters* (Atlanta, 1989). Also, for the New Testament: Stephen Neill, *The Interpretation of the New Testament, 1861–1986*, Second Edition by Tom Wright (Oxford, 1988).

Related texts

The essential work on ancient Near Eastern texts is James B. Pritchard, *Ancient Near Eastern Texts Relating to the Old Testament*, Third Edition with Supplement (Princeton, 1969). For the Jewish 'intertestamental literature' (other than the Apocrypha) the standard collection is now James H. Charlesworth, ed., *The Old Testament Pseudepigrapha* (New York, 2 vols., 1983–5). For the Dead Sea Scrolls, see Geza Vermes, *The Dead Sea Scrolls in English*, Third Edition (Harmondsworth, 1987).

History of interpretation

The most comprehensive work is Peter R. Ackroyd and C. F. Evans, eds., *The Cambridge History of the Bible* (Cambridge, 3 vols., 1963–70). Many of the issues raised in the present book are discussed at greater length in Stephen Prickett, *Words and the Word: Language, Poetics and Biblical Interpretation* (Cambridge, 1986) and will be discussed further in Stephen Prickett, ed., *Reading the Text: Biblical Interpretation and Literary Theory* (Oxford, 1991). An up-to-date account of the various modes of contemporary Biblical interpretation is Robert Morgan and John Barton, *Biblical Interpretation* (Oxford, 1988). Outstanding recent works on the Bible as literature include Northrop Frye, *The Great Code: the Bible and Literature* (London, 1982) and Gabriel Josipovici, *The Book of God: a Response to the Bible* (New Haven, Conn., 1988). Much light is thrown on the Authorized Version by John Bois, *Translating for King James: Being a True Copy of the Only Notes made by a Translator of the King James Version* (ed. and trans. by Ward Allen, London, 1970).